STOP BEATING THE DEAD HORSE

WHY THE SYSTEM OF PUBLIC EDUCATION IN
THE UNITED STATES HAS FAILED
AND
WHAT TO DO ABOUT IT

Edition II

BY

JULIE L. CASEY, B.S.Ed

With JONN T. CASEY, M.A.Ed

Copyright © 2010 by Julie L. Casey
ISBN 978-0-557-47045-7

Cover design and photo by Amanda S. Eldridge

ISBN 978-0615988443

All rights reserved. No part of this book may be used or reproduced in any manner without the written permission of the publisher.

Printed in the United States of America.

For more information, visit
www.stopbeatingthedeadhorse.com.

To the thousands of dedicated and talented teachers, including my wonderful husband Jonn and dear friends Christina and Doc, who must deal with the frustrations and problems of the current system of public education, with apathetic, unprepared, and sometimes sullen students, and with piles of paperwork and red tape, yet still manage to impart knowledge and compassion to their students.

Also to my children and my now and future grandchildren for whom I hope the public education system will be greatly improved.

Acknowledgments

I am so grateful to my family and friends who have supported me through the process of writing this book, especially those trusted and beloved ones who served as peer editors: Jonn Casey, Lee Powell, Jan Powell, Myrna Hopkins, John and Linda Casey, "Doc" Pilgram, and especially my lovely and intelligent sister, Amanda Eldridge, whose thoughts and questions helped me to refine my ideas and present them more clearly.

I would also like to thank, from the bottom of my heart, all the teachers, past and present, who have made a difference in my life, the lives of my children, and the lives of the American people.

Contents

Introduction		1
<u>Section 1</u>	The Problems (The Dead Horse)	3
Chapter 1	The Root of the Problems (Who Killed the Horse?)	5
Chapter 2	Consequences of a Failed System (She's Pregnant; He's an Addict: What Went Wrong?)	21
Chapter 3	The Fundamental Problems with the Current System (The Same Old Horse)	52
<u>Section 2</u>	The Solutions (A New Horse!)	67
Chapter 4	The Level Mastery System (A Horse of a Different Color)	69
Chapter 5	How the Level Mastery System Addresses the Fundamental Problems of the Current System (What to Look for When Buying a New Horse)	79
Chapter 6	Basic Structure of the Level Mastery System (Equine Conformation)	87
Chapter 7	Curriculum for the Basic Diploma (Learning to Ride Your New Horse)	99
Chapter 8	Curricula for the Advanced Diploma (Now You're Ready for the Show)	105
Chapter 9	Financing the Level Mastery System	109

	Stop Beating the Dead Horse (Betting on the New Horse)	ii
Chapter 10	How to Get Started (First, Place Your Foot in the Stirrup)	117

Appendices   119

Figure 1	Sample Personalized Progress Summary	121
Figure 2	Sample Contents of Level Packet and Corresponding Software Links	123
Figure 3	Sample Classroom Layout 1	125
Figure 4	Sample Classroom Layout 2	127
Figure 5	Sample Website for Voting on Basic Diploma Curriculum	129

References   131

Introduction

A lot of people these days talk about how the public school system in the United States does not work. They propose endless solutions to fix the system. They give new names to old ideas and throw around clever catch phrases to intrigue their audience. But the United States system of public education is not "broken" and therefore cannot be fixed: it is simply the wrong system for education in the United States today. The system was designed for the convenience of the "shopkeepers," to make it easier to sort, manage, control, force conformity, and institutionalize these "unruly creatures" we call children. How and why was it decided that children should be lumped together by age? How was the curriculum decided upon? Were there any studies done back in the early to mid 19th century, when the system was beginning to take shape, to figure out how children learn and what they need to learn to function reasonably in society? If so, did the founding powers-that-be pay heed to the results of those studies? Has anyone stopped to really question the basic setup of the system?

When I started thinking about what was wrong with the public school system back in the early 1980s, after completing my bachelor of science in elementary education, I was thinking along the lines that most people do: what can be done to *improve* the system, what can be done to *increase the knowledge* of the students, what can be done to *increase their test scores*. Then a few years ago when I was homeschooling my own four sons, it hit me – the problem is that the public school system was designed in a way that is counterproductive to the way children learn.

Education experts today know how children learn. Strategies are attempted to implement this knowledge in the system to no avail. The reason for this is that the system works against learning on an individual level. For example, inquiry-based learning, a technique in which the student asks and seeks answers to questions in order to learn a subject, is a wonderful approach to education, one I use constantly in homeschooling my children, but it is difficult to fully implement in the traditional public school setting. A class of twenty students individually inquiring and seeking knowledge at their own pace is unruly and hard to manage in the current system. The inquiry-based learning techniques must be squeezed and tweaked and restricted to keep all twenty students at generally the same place in knowledge of the subject at all times. This discourages students from truly gaining knowledge through inquiry. When they know they will not be encouraged to pursue a subject that interests them, beyond what their classmates are learning, the joy, and therefore the benefit, of inquiry is squelched.

I want to make it clear, from the beginning, that this book is not an indictment of any person or group of people involved in education today. The purpose of this book is to show that the system known today as the public school system of the United States does not work and could never work, *why* it does not work, and to propose an alternative system that could be implemented in its place.

SECTION 1: THE PROBLEMS
(The Dead Horse)

Stop Beating the Dead Horse 4

One

The Root of the Problems
(Who Killed the Horse?)

Dakota tribal wisdom says that when you discover you are riding a dead horse, the best strategy is to dismount. In regards to the system of public education, however, lawmakers and educators often try other strategies for fixing the dead horse (a.k.a. public schooling), including the following:

1. Buying a stronger whip.
2. Changing riders.
3. Saying things like, "This is the way we have always ridden this horse."
4. Appointing a committee to study the horse.
5. Arranging to visit other countries to see how other cultures ride dead horses.
6. Lowering the standards to include dead horses.
7. Reclassifying the dead horse as living-impaired.
8. Creating a training session to increase our riding ability.
9. Comparing the state of dead horses in today's environment.
10. Harnessing several dead horses together for increased speed.

11. Providing additional funding to increase the horse's performance.
12. Doing a productivity study to see if lighter riders can increase the dead horse's performance.
13. Purchasing technology to make dead horses run faster.
14. Rewriting the expected performance requirements for all horses.

People like to blame *someone* for problems. Many people blame the president, Congress, local school boards, administrators, or teachers for the shortfalls of the public school system. The problem is not that the educators and lawmakers aren't trying to improve the system; it's that they just haven't realized the proverbial horse is dead. If the basic system doesn't work, all the money and strategies and dedication in the world will not help unless the system itself is replaced.

What the United States Public School System is Doing Right

In spite of all the problems in the current system, there are some important things that the educators and lawmakers are doing right. To begin with, they recognize that something is wrong and continue to pursue answers. Although I believe their attempts are misguided, at least the effort is there. Education is at the forefront of the issues facing politicians today. Much time and a lot of money have been spent and continue to be pledged in order to find solutions.

Also, I find that the vast majority of the people associated with schools, as well as lawmakers, care deeply about children and their education. They work hard, sometimes passionately, to figure out the best solutions to help students. All their hard work and dedication falls short, however, because the basic system stays the same. The problem doesn't lie with the people charged to fix the system; the problem is *the system itself*.

Furthermore, teachers are well trained and well prepared to teach. Back in the 1980s teacher qualification was a real issue. A small percentage of teachers were poorly trained (or not trained at all, having begun their careers before certification was required) and substandard. Thanks to public funding and an overhaul of the requirements for teaching, that is no longer a real problem in the system. Yet still the education of our students is not at par with many other industrialized nations because, regardless of the quality of our teachers, they still must teach within the confines of an inferior system.

Offering choices, such as charter schools, private and parochial schools, and homeschooling, to parents and students is another significant thing that lawmakers and educators are doing right. Charles Murray, best-selling author of <u>Real Education: Four Simple Truths for Bringing America's School Back to Reality</u>, says,

> *"The reason private schools, charter schools, and home-schooling are desirable is their ability to create a better education in ways that do not show up in reading and math scores."* [1]

Charter schools operate as autonomous public schools which are accountable for student performance in exchange for public funding. The charter school format allows for innovation in education that cannot be implemented within the confines and regulations of traditional public schools. These schools provide an important testing ground for those seeking answers to the shortcomings of the system. They also offer a variety of teaching strategies and curricula to best fit the needs of the students they serve.

Only through options like these can new ideas and learning strategies be implemented and tested as to their effectiveness. According to many studies, as well as anecdotal evidence from parents, the students taking advantage of the aforementioned options often fare better academically and intrinsically than their traditionally schooled peers.

What the Public School System is Doing Wrong

The current system of public schooling in the United States came about in the mid 1800s and early 1900s. Horace Mann, who is often referred to as the "The Father of American Education" believed that public education would be a great equalizer, not only in economic and social class, but in race and gender, as well. He also believed that a common education in a common school would create good citizens, unite society and prevent crime and poverty. Mann became Massachusetts's first secretary of education and was able to advance his ideas and ideals to induce both government and private sectors into investing in a public education system. His success propelled other states to adopt similar policies. By 1918, every state in the union had laws requiring all children to attend at least elementary school.

In the beginning, Mann patterned his design for a public education system after the 18th century Prussian model which divided students by age and required compulsory attendance, national training for teachers, national testing for all students (to classify students for potential job training), a national curriculum, and mandatory kindergarten. These components were created to instill social obedience in the citizens through indoctrination. In the United States, many proponents of a compulsory public education system had similar ideas for the purpose of such a system. Benjamin Rush, a signer of the Declaration of Independence and ardent supporter of publicly funded schools, wrote,

> *"Our schools of learning, by producing one general and uniform system of education, will render the mass of the people more homogeneous and thereby fit them more easily for uniform and peaceable government...Let our pupil be taught that he does not belong to himself, but that he is public property...The authority of our masters [should] be as absolute as possible...By this mode of education, we prepare our youth for the subordination of laws and thereby qualify them for becoming good citizens of the republic."*

In 1816 Archibald D. Murphey, founder of the North Carolina public schools, wrote:

> *"In these schools the precepts of morality and religion should be inculcated, and habits of subordination and obedience be formed."*

It is particularly interesting that the word "inculcate" is often used in reference to educating children in the early days of public schooling. To inculcate means to fix something firmly in somebody's mind through frequent, forceful repetition.

In a similar vein, Noah Webster believed that

> "*good republicans ... are formed by a singular machinery in the body politic, which takes the child as soon as he can speak, checks his natural independence and passions, makes him subordinate to superior age, to the laws of the state, to town and parochial institutions.*"

William T. Harris, U.S. Commissioner of Education in 1889, said,

> "*Our schools have been scientifically designed to prevent over-education from happening. The average American [should be] content with their humble role in life, because they're not tempted to think about any other role.*"

Some parents in the early days of forced public schooling were opposed, sometimes vehemently, to the compulsory nature of it. They sensed, even then, that their rights as parents to be able to decide what was best for their children would be undermined. They could foresee the deterioration of their influence on their children's lives and many felt that their values would not be passed on to their children through a public institution such as school. In some places, compulsory public schooling had to be forcefully imposed upon the citizens by the police and/or military. Many of these parents realized that if making school affordable for everyone were the only goal, the early public school organizers would have simply given tuition grants to needy families, which would have been much more efficient and less expensive: however, it would not have given the organizers the social control of the masses they desired. I wonder if that isn't the real reason behind the opposition to school vouchers even today.

The components of the model used in the system today to educate students – dividing students by age, separating lessons into disconnected tasks, making teachers the center of focus in the classrooms, requiring standardized testing, providing meals and after-school activities such as sports and other non-academic diversions – cannot be found in any other part of life. Not in our family lives, our working lives, our community lives, nor our spiritual lives are we ever subjected to all of the following: being segregated by age, our tasks separated and regulated by bells, central authority figures having total control over all our thoughts and actions, meals and extracurricular activities being provided for us, being compelled by law to attend, and being tested regularly to compare us to our peers of the same age. Only in the context of the institution of public school do all these unlike-real-life circumstances exist together. They do not serve to prepare the student for real life; they merely control the students while they are in that institution. They are similar only to the circumstances one finds oneself in while in another institution – prison. As William Glasser, a noted American psychiatrist, said,

> *"There are only two places in the world where time takes precedence over the job to be done. School and prison."*

George Bernard Shaw wrote,

> *"[School] is a prison. But it is in some respects more cruel than a prison. In a*

prison, for instance, you are not forced to read books written by the warder and the governor."

Some may argue that the military and factory work are similar to the institution of public schooling. While that may be true, I would point out two important observations: 1) joining the military and working in a factory are not compulsory, as is school, and 2) if the military or factory work are the closest real-life situations to public schooling (besides prison), is that what we want our education system to be geared for – training only military and factory workers – and does that training really take thirteen years to accomplish?

Much of a regular school day in a typical elementary school is spent waiting in lines. Students must wait in lines to go to recess, they wait in lines to go to lunch, more lines to use the bathroom, to get a drink from the fountain, to go to P.E., to go to music; their day starts out waiting in line to get on the school bus and ends waiting in line to get back on the school bus. I have personally observed that up to 20% (and probably more) of the school day in elementary school is spent waiting in lines. Administrators and teachers say this is a necessary way to maintain discipline and this is probably true in the current system, which models itself after a prison and assumes that students cannot possibly have the self-control to move about and use the toilet on their own. Think about how much you hate waiting in a line for ten minutes, then multiply that by eight – this is how long students wait in line on a typical day in a typical school. It's no wonder they are antsy and fidgety all day. It's no wonder that many are angry by the time they are teenagers. Why do we unthinkingly subject our children to things we would not be willing to do as adults?

Most of the components of our current system, however, were not always the norm. They came about over time, as a result of this study or that, or for the convenience of the system. For example, students in the United States were originally only required to attend school from the ages of 8 to 14 and for only three months a year. Schools were most often one-room schools, in which children of all ages worked on their own lessons and helped younger students as needed. Providing meals to students did not begin until the mid 1900s and was instituted as a result of studies that showed students learn better when well fed, so instead of giving families the means to feed their own children, the educational system took that responsibility on itself. In the early to mid 1900s schools started offering sports and other hobbies in order to direct and control the free time of students in diversions which were deemed acceptable by the church and community leaders. In the ensuing years, adult-directed activities for children became the norm to the extent that, today, children don't know how to play on their own like they used to. Our current system has evolved over a hundred and fifty years or so into a behemoth that goes way beyond its original purpose of educating and equalizing the masses. Sir Winston Churchill wrote,

> *"Schools have not necessarily much to do with education... they are mainly institutions of control, where basic habits must be inculcated in the young. Education is quite different and has little place in school."*

John Taylor Gatto, three-time New York City Teacher of the Year and 1991 New York State Teacher of the Year, claims,

> *"The truth is that schools don't really teach anything except how to obey orders."*[2]

What does all this history serve to tell us about why the current system does not work? It explains that the system was not created to educate students in the most effective way; rather, it began as a way to force conformity and civil obedience. It shows that the various components that make the system up today were added at random, in hodge-podge fashion, with little thought to the future consequences, the total educational value to students, or the compatibility to the whole system. It illustrates that control and order are the underlying motives for the way the system is set up. It tells us that the system was never designed to enable students to excel in education, just to equalize them.

H. L. Mencken, an American writer of the early twentieth century, wrote,

> *"The aim of public education is not to spread enlightenment at all, it is simply to reduce as many individuals as possible to the same safe level, to breed and train a standardized citizenry, to put down dissent and originality."*

That may have been a good, and even noble, endeavor in the early days of public education when masses of immigrants were arriving, all speaking different languages and with vastly different ideas of what a country and a government should be, but it no longer works in today's global and technological society. It is the wrong system for education today. The system needs to be replaced, not revamped.

Why Some Students Succeed in the Current System

Many students succeed in the current system as defined by that system: virtually all students who stay in school through the 12th grade graduate; many go on to college; most get jobs; most become members of society who contribute in some way; most are not criminals or drug addicts. In this context of success, most students do succeed.

But I'm not referring to the students who succeed as a product of the system. My reference is to the few students who succeed in spite of the system. By succeed, I mean those students who graduate with their sense of independence, self-worth, creativity, and thirst for knowledge intact. These students aren't always the ones graduating with high marks; on the contrary, they are often ones who have played the public school game just adequately enough to get by, biding their time until they can be free, then making the most of that freedom to pursue what really interests them. They make their own success in the world, make their own choices, and "own" their future. They are the kind of people who have an inner drive, an insatiable curiosity, a desire to pursue something more than what is taught in school. These are the people who become entrepreneurs instead of merely workers and consumers. These are the people who find ways to move science and technology forward. These are the people who become icons in their fields. They are the Bill Gateses, the Oprah Winfreys, the Donald Trumps, the Martha Stewarts, the Ted Turners.

Why Many More Don't Succeed

Unfortunately, truly successful people are getting fewer and fewer in the United States. The traits of the successful adult (independence, creativity, high energy, inquisitiveness, motivation, joy) are discouraged and suppressed in the current system because they create unruliness and disorder in the system. John Dewey, a progressive educational reformer of the late 1800s and early 1900s declared that

> *"children who know how to think for themselves spoil the harmony of the collective society which is coming where everyone is interdependent."*

By suppressing these traits, we are, by default, preventing truly successful adulthood. It is but a few rare individuals, usually those with strong familial support, who are able to overcome this repression of spirit and find real success in adulthood.

I believe that most students in our country *can* succeed in a meaningful way in adulthood, given a system of education that encourages the traits of a successful adult. In the current system, however, this could never become a reality. This system encourages dependency, immaturity, irresponsibility, and mediocrity.

It is interesting to note that many of the great scientists, writers, and intellectuals of the modern era were either homeschooled or self-taught, to some extent, in their elementary and secondary years. Most were not taught in an institutional setting for their entire school careers, even though schools were available to them: Benjamin Franklin, Thomas Alva Edison, Alexander Graham Bell, Cyrus McCormick, Orville and Wilbur Wright, Margaret Meade, Beatrix Potter, Agatha Christie, and Albert Einstein, to name a few. Franklin's family could only afford to send him to school for two years, after which he educated himself by reading voraciously. Edison, who was hearing impaired, was labeled a misfit and "addled" by the institution he attended for only three months; thereafter, he was homeschooled by his mother, who was certain of her son's intelligence. Bell was homeschooled until the age of ten: he then attended school for just three years. Cyrus McCormick, the inventor of the first commercial reaper, and Orville and Wilbur Wright were entirely homeschooled.

Margaret Mead, American cultural anthropologist and author, wrote

> *"My grandmother wanted me to have an education, so she kept me out of school."*

Beatrix Potter, who is best known for her wildly popular series of children's books and who was also a respected scientist, said,

> *"Thank goodness I was never sent to school; it would have rubbed off some of the originality."*

Albert Einstein was enrolled in the Prussian compulsory institutions of learning but studied mathematics and reasoning on his own. In secondary school, Einstein was in constant conflict with school authorities and resented the confinement of school regimen. About school, he later wrote,

> *"One had to cram all this stuff into one's mind, whether one liked it or not. This coercion had such a deterring effect that, after I had passed the final examination, I found the consideration of any scientific problems distasteful to me for an entire year.... It is in fact nothing short of a*

miracle that the modern methods of instruction have not yet entirely strangled the holy curiosity of inquiry."

Like Einstein, many of the intellectuals who were publicly schooled were less than satisfied about their educational experiences. Mark Twain, who seemed particularly discontented with his experiences in public school, said,

"I have never let my schooling interfere with my education."

George Bernard Shaw wrote,

"My schooling not only failed to teach me what it professed to be teaching, but prevented me from being educated to an extent which infuriates me when I think of all I might have learned at home by myself."

Ralph Waldo Emerson stated,

"We are students of words; we are shut up in schools, and colleges, and recitation rooms, for ten or fifteen years, and come out at last with a bag of wind, a memory of words, and do not know a thing."

It seems that the freedom of homeschooling or self-teaching allows one to think outside the box, so to speak, to see things in a different way, to approach problems from a different point of view. Of course, many great scientists attended institutions of learning, but I would venture to say that most, if not all, like Einstein, pursued knowledge outside of the institutional setting as well. One can only wonder at the turn of events in the world of science and technology had these great scientists not possessed the means or wherewithal to educate themselves, but instead, been forced to rely on an institution to give them the knowledge and creativity needed to form their ideas.

What's at Stake for the United States?

Almost everyone knows these days that the United States ranks very low among industrialized nations of the world in math and science. Those scores, in themselves, do not mean that our country is in danger of being eclipsed by other countries that are better educated than we are. They do, however, prove that our system is favoring quantity over quality in education and that equalizing students rather than bringing out the best in each student is the goal of our system. It shows that we are limiting our potential and stifling our human resources, that we actively seek mediocrity.

Our culture is also eroding to the point where crime and violence have become the norm in some places. A country which must expend much of its valuable resources to maintain order and peace is not going to remain on top for long. The deterioration of family and community life is rampant everywhere. Without these basics of human need, the quality of life sharply declines. The public school system encourages the deterioration of the family and community and instigates the anger and despair that fuels crime and violence. It is ironic that the very system that was created to control the masses and force obedience and morality – the public school system – has failed miserably at those basic functions. The system disregards human nature, just as communism does, and so was destined to fail even before it began.

Albert Shanker, former president of the American Federation of Teachers, stated that

> *"it is time to admit that public education...more resembles a Communist economy than our own market economy."*

A simplified definition of communism is a scheme of equalizing the social conditions of life. A communist state is generally run by an authoritarian form of government in which its citizens are told how to live. In these ways, the public education system is run like a communist state. The problem with communism, as well as with our school system, is that people are not equal in their natures; they have an amazing array of different levels of intelligence, energy, industry, interests, values, hopes and dreams; people, even children, recognize this about themselves and others, and many rebel at the idea of being homogenized. When a system seeks to equalize human beings who are by their very nature unequal (that is, in personality, not human rights), the system cannot hope to thrive. The ideal of equalizing the masses through education seems a good idea but, in reality, is impossible and undesirable. One of the most crucial things the system has failed to do is differentiate between equal educational opportunity for all and equal (or identical) education for all. Instead of trying to make everybody the same, an educational system must ensure equal rights for everyone while still allowing them to develop at their own rate and in their own way. Only then can we have the diversity, creativity, and ingenuity needed to compete in the world today.

Two

Consequences of a Failed System
(She's Pregnant; He's an Addict What Went Wrong?)

The focus of education today must be reexamined to determine what we, as a country, want from our system of education. In the past, the system has been focused on socialization and homogenization of our citizens. This focus has not only failed to educate our students well in the basics of reading, writing, and arithmetic but, most importantly, it has also failed to prepare them for life. An unknown, but wise, author, wrote,

> *"An educational system isn't worth a great deal if it teaches young people how to make a living but doesn't teach them how to make a life."*

Many of this country's current social problems would not be happening (the mortgage crisis, surging unemployment rates, rising teen violence, irresponsible parenting, preventable vehicle deaths, etc.) if the system had been educating students to prepare them for life. In the public school setting, we have a great opportunity to address these problems and any other problems which may arise, and educate students to prevent them in the future. It is very important that any system of education be flexible enough to change as the educational needs of society change. The inflexibility of our current system has been a major problem of education in the United States today. Our current system is using the methods and curriculum developed for an early industrial age to educate students for the entirely different world of today.

Deterioration of the Family Unit

It is no wonder that there is a weakening of what was known as the family unit. In days long gone by, the family unit consisted of two parents, children, and often extended family members such as grandparents and cousins. Families were together for a large part of each day, often working together, playing together, and always eating together. Children played with their siblings, shared a room, sometimes even slept in the same bed with them, and shared the same toys. Parents taught their children what they needed to know to get by in the world. Children respected their parents and trusted them to steer them right. Grandparents were especially respected for their knowledge and wisdom. Families generally got along with each other, enjoyed being together, and, indeed, treasured each other.

Fast forward to today's family. Today's family may consist of parents and their children, many times only one parent, or sometimes a grandparent raising a grandchild without the parents' involvement. Today's family spends most of the day apart, with parents working and children going to school or day care. Often, they spend an average of only two or three hours a day together. Parents entrust the education of their children to institutions instead of teaching them themselves. Children mistrust their parents, roll their eyes at them, and rebel against them. They feel their parents can't possibly understand what they're going through, mainly because they really don't know each other very well. Today's family often eats breakfast on the run, lunch apart from each other, and supper together only if their various schedules will allow. Siblings often fight and vie for their parents' limited attention; they have playmates from school and don't like playing with their siblings; they have their own bedrooms and their own toys which they do not share with their brothers and sisters. Grandparents, though loved, are often thought of as old-fashioned and out of touch with the world and therefore not worth listening to. When the grandparents can't care for themselves, they are sent to an institution for care, instead of into the arms of the family they raised. Today's family treasures independence and encourages separateness.

It's no secret how all these changes came about. With industrialization came the need for workers. Women entered the workforce and their children had to be cared for by someone else. Some people believe that public schools were instituted for the sake of industry for two reasons: it provided free babysitting so that women could be free to work outside the home, and it provided a training ground for future workers who would be required to work in large groups and not do too much thinking on their own. Other people believe an additional goal for public schools was to create a nation of consumers to drive the industrial age. Early industrialists such as John D. Rockefeller and Andrew Carnegie spent huge sums of money (actually more than the government did at that time) on public schooling between 1900 and 1920.[1] Their actions may have been purely altruistic or may have had an underlying purpose.

Whether or not public schooling was started for the sake of industry, the reality is that it separates children from their parents, both physically and emotionally. The system, in recent years, has been trying to separate children from their parents at earlier and earlier ages. In the 1800s, the average age for beginning compulsory school attendance was eight years old: by the year 2000 the age requirement was lowered to five or six in over half the states. In the other states, even though attendance isn't compulsory until later, usually age seven, it is universally accepted that children start school at the age of five or six.

Additionally, educators strongly encourage parents to send their children to preschool programs as early as two and three years old, claiming that these programs will greatly improve their children's future success in school. Many people take for granted that this claim is true (though there is substantial evidence to the contrary): however there is no doubt that separating children from their parents at this critical age has detrimental effects in the children's development of emotional attachments. Karl Zinsmeister, adjunct research associate at the American Enterprise Institute for Public Policy Research, says,

> *"Declining parental attachment is an extremely serious risk to children today. The verdict of enormous psychological literature is that time spent with a parent is the very clearest correlate of healthy child development."*[2]

This may be the precise reason that children who attend preschool seem to do better in school – they have been taken away from their families before they become too emotionally attached and before they learn to think for themselves: therefore they are easier to control in school. While this may help children perform in the current system, it does not prepare them for a life after school; they are not equipped with the solid foundation of parental attachment needed to form meaningful relationships later in life. They learn that an institution is a better parent than their own parents, or themselves when they become parents, and they pass along this idea of inadequate parenting to their children, as well.

After reading the words of the founding fathers of public education, there can be little doubt that a major goal was to usurp parental control of children. Archibald D. Murphey, founder of the North Carolina public schools, stated,

> *"Their parents know not how to instruct them.... The state, in the warmth of her affection and solicitude for their welfare, must take charge of those children and place them in school where their minds can be enlightened and their hearts trained to virtue."*

John Swett, superintendent of California Public School System in the 1860s, wrote,

> *"[T]he child should be taught to consider his instructor...superior to the parent in point of authority.... The vulgar impression that parents have a legal right to dictate to teachers is entirely erroneous.... Parents have no remedy as against the teacher."*

More recently, the Association of California School Administrators declared,

> *"'Parent choice' proceeds from the belief that the purpose of education is to provide individual students with an education. In fact, educating the individual is but a means to the true end of education, which is to*

create a viable social order to which individuals contribute and by which they are sustained."

The first mission statement of Rockefeller's General Education Board in 1906 ended with these words:

"We will organize children and teach them in a perfect way the things their fathers and mothers are doing in an imperfect way."

Horace Mann believed,

"We who are engaged in the sacred cause of education are entitled to look upon all parents as having given hostages to our cause."

We need a system of education today that gives children back to their families, respects parental rights, and involves the family in education. Of course, the first task of such a system would have to be to educate students and parents in how to be parents again, while at the same time reinstating not only their rights, but their responsibilities as parents.

Irresponsible Parenting

When I was young, parents were responsible for sending their children to school sustained by a good night's sleep and a good breakfast, armed with a nutritious lunch, clad in clean and adequate clothing, equipped with all necessary school supplies, and admonished that if they misbehaved, they'd "get it twice as bad" when they got home. These days, many of these parental responsibilities have been supplanted by the system, ostensibly to ensure better education. But I suspect it is equally done to replace the child's need for a parent and in some instances, for the monetary gain of school districts. When my older children were in public school, letters were sent home at the beginning of every school year urging parents to apply for free or reduced lunch and breakfast. While this strategy may help to feed underprivileged students, thereby helping them learn in the short run, the real lesson being taught here is that the parents do not have to be responsible for feeding their children. Some schools even have programs, such as "Backpack Buddies," that send nutritious food home for underprivileged students on the weekends.[3] Many schools that serve underprivileged students have a clothes closet or work with local charities to provide pieces of clothing to inadequately clothed students. Some schools even offer medical exams from professionals who come to the schools so that parents do not have to take their children to the doctor or dentist for checkups. While all these programs seem worthy and advantageous on the surface, there is a dark side to taking over parental responsibilities. With all the help from public schools, – meals, clothes closets, medical exams, bussing, etc. – parents barely have to parent at all any more and too many take advantage of this. And the worst thing about this is that their children are learning that they won't have to be responsible parents in the future because they know the system will take care of their children, as well.

The public school system needs to be stripped of all parental responsibilities, and those responsibilities must be put back on the parents. This means that the system will be out of the restaurant business. No more space needs to be wasted on cafeterias; there's no reason students can't eat their sack lunches from home in a classroom (then clean up after themselves!) or even eat lunch with their parents off-campus, if possible. There is no scientific or nutritional reason to require a hot meal, but if the temperature of their child's meal is important to parents for some psychological reason, hot meals from home can be brought in a thermos. No more money needs to be spent on cafeteria workers, food, refrigerators, ovens, tables, trays, silverware, etc. If a parent cannot afford to send a sack lunch (though I find that hard to believe, since a PB&J sandwich and an apple can be bought for pennies), that family can be referred to Social Services for help. Most poor families can make use of governmental programs such as WIC and food stamps, but it takes some effort from the parents to get on those programs and effort from the parents is what shows responsibility.

When the system takes over the responsibility of feeding their children, parents sometimes spend their money on unnecessary items such as cigarettes, cell phones, video games, etc. My husband worked at a low-income public high school where three-quarters of the students were on free or reduced lunch, yet most of these same students had cell phones and drove newer vehicles than he did. A large number of the students and their parents smoked, as well. Many did illegal drugs – in fact, a methamphetamine lab blew up two blocks from the school one day and everybody had to be evacuated. People have money for illegal, unhealthy, and unnecessary items because they are not forced to provide the basic needs, such as food, clothing, and medical care, for their children.

Now, I know what some people will say: the children will suffer because their parents won't take their parental responsibility seriously. That is when the school refers neglectful parents to Social Services, and that agency deals with it. In the meantime, a jar of peanut butter, a loaf of bread, and some apples on hand keep the child from starving while waiting for Social Services to do their job. My mother, who worked as a school nurse in a low income school in the public school system for fifteen years, believed there should be a checklist of parental responsibilities that the school would check off as completed by the parent, and, if in compliance, the checklist would be turned over to the state before a welfare check is issued. This might be something to look into, at least until parents have relearned and reclaimed their parental responsibilities.

Another facet to making responsible parents is to teach parenting to all students, since most will likely grow up to be parents. I don't mean a semester of "Home Ec" or "Family Living." I mean ongoing parenting and family living skills from early childhood through graduation taught in schools and mirrored by the students' own parents taking on their parental responsibilities. These living skills include, but are not limited to, being a good parent, learning how to make nutritious food choices, preventing unwanted pregnancies, living harmoniously with others, keeping a house clean, etc. After a generation or two of teaching these skills, it may be appropriate to phase them out of the curriculum because parents will be passing on these skills to their children, as is the natural scheme of things.

Teen Attitudes and Unsocial Behavior

How nice would it be if all the teenagers working at the local burger joint were courteous and friendly as they correctly count back your change? The fact that we, as a society, *accept* that teenagers act the way they do now is the precise reason they do. There is no real reason that we must accept, and therefore *condone* this behavior and dismiss it as some kind of biological milestone in a person's life; it isn't. Sure, teenagers feel rebellious and are striving for independence, but that does not excuse belligerence and downright unsocial behavior. Teens should be responsible for their future, they should "own" their lives, they should have independence and control in one of the most important parts of their lives – their education. If the public education system allowed these things to occur, I believe that incidences of rebellion would drop dramatically, teen anger would be dissipated, and their attitudes would improve. And with the teaching of (and insistence upon) good manners in school, teens would be more courteous without even thinking about it.

Unsocial behavior among teens is becoming more and more of a problem. Many high school graduates do not know how to communicate with adults, handicapping them in their jobs and their lives. I believe the public school system is the prime cause of this problem. It creates an environment that is counter-productive to true socialization. Many opponents of homeschooling (the National Education Association in particular) cite the lack of socialization as a key disadvantage of learning at home. They believe that institutionalizing children – forcing them to socialize only with other children of the same age and usually the same general socio-economic background, often further dividing them by gender (as in boys' line and girls' line, boys against girls, boys' sports and girls' sports, etc.), and being dictated to by adults who are seen, not as social peers, but as authoritative figures – is conducive to true social behavior. Publicly schooled children in general are not social, they are socialized; the difference being in the quality of the social connections they are permitted to make. Outside of public school, people are free to associate with other people of all ages, genders, races, and socio-economic backgrounds. In this way, a person learns to be social with all types of people. Homeschooled children are consistently more social with adults and more accepting of gender and race differences than their publicly schooled counterparts because of this freedom to associate with a wide variety of people. A study by the Fraser Institute, an independent public policy organization, found that the typical homeschooled child is more mature, friendly, happy, thoughtful, competent, less peer dependent, better socialized, and exhibits "significantly higher" self-esteem than students in public or private schools.[4] ERIC, the Education Resources Information Center of the U.S. government, which has published multiple articles on homeschooling, reports that

> *"insofar as self concept is a reflector of socialization, ... there may be sufficient evidence to indicate that some home-schooled children have a higher self concept than conventionally schooled children."* [5]

This doesn't mean that the only way to improve social behavior in our children is to homeschool them. A new system of public schooling can be created to implement this. To be effective in encouraging social behavior in children, a public school system must allow for the freedom to associate with people of all ages, separation by gender needs to be eliminated (except, obviously, in bathrooms), and teachers and administrators need to be mentors and advocates, someone a child can trust and relate to, not someone to be subjugated to.

Teen Violence

Incidences of violence, and especially teen violence, are much more prevalent now than, say, fifty years ago. Or even forty, or even twenty. Annual statistics show that the United States is not as safe as it used to be for young people. Homicide is the second leading cause of death among teens, second only to accidents. Suicide, which is violence committed on oneself, is the third leading cause of death among teens. Violence has escalated, especially in our schools; incidences of bullying (taken to new heights with cyber bullying), school shootings, bomb threats, and gang activity in the schools are frightening. Many of these problems arise from unhappy students who don't want to be at school; they feel school is irrelevant to their lives and that it is an imposition on them to be forced to attend. Many have learning problems that are not addressed, whether it is above-average intelligence (causing boredom and inattention), learning disabilities, or physical problems such as mental disorders and hyperactivity (which will be discussed later). Many problems are caused by irresponsible and unresponsive parents. Often times, it is a combination of several of these factors that lead to increased violence and suicide.

In his book <u>The Conspiracy of Ignorance: The Failure of the American Public Schools</u>, Martin L. Gross contends that

> *"[public high school] has denied teenagers the chance to come of age intellectually as well as biologically. Once that opportunity is lost, as it usually is today, it can seldom be recaptured..."*[6]

Teens, at least by the age of sixteen or so, are biologically and physically adults. The reason that most are not prepared emotionally and mentally for adulthood is that the current educational system, as well as our society, encourages them to remain helpless, dependent, and immature. They have no real responsibilities in life, they are given possessions they should be earning, and they are indulged, yet they are not trusted with making decisions for themselves. A hundred years ago, people were on their own by the age of fifteen or sixteen, working, making their place in the community, and starting families. Now they are forced to languish for several years in a setting that is at odds with their biological clocks, making them restless, unhappy, surly, and angry.

Dr. Robert Epstein, in his book <u>The Case Against Adolescence: Rediscovering the Adult in Every Teen</u>, contends that this anger, and therefore the violence, is caused by artificially extending childhood well past puberty. He makes the point that throughout human history, up until the last century, people were considered adults and treated as such shortly after puberty. He also notes that there were very few problems associated with teens until the last 50 or 60 years, which just so happens to coincide with the extension of the compulsory school attendance age to at least 16. A study conducted by Dr. Epstein and Diane Dumas recently revealed that

> *"teens appear to be subjected to about twice as many restrictions as are prisoners and soldiers and to more than ten times as many restrictions as are everyday adults."* [7]

Teens react to this subjugation with rebellion, anger, depression, or passivity. None of these reactions are healthy.

Our culture, as well as our school system, needs to recognize teens as young adults and to equip them with the skills to be responsible and independent instead of being an ever-increasing drag on society. We need a system that will make use of the enormous energy and creativity that can be found in people of this age group.

Teen Pregnancy

The United States has the highest rate of teen pregnancies in the industrialized world, although the number of teen pregnancies has been dropping since the 1950s, from an all time high of 96 births per 1,000 women aged 15-19 in 1957 to an all time low of 49 per 1,000 in the year 2000. This statistic is misleading, though. More importantly, is how many *non-marital* births are occurring in the teen years. In the 1950s only 13% of teen births were non-marital, whereas the number is around 79% today.[8] This statistic shows that more and more teenage girls are having children outside of marriage, which is a much more socially troubling statistic for our society.

The high teen birth rate in 1957 corresponded with an equally high rate of teen marriage at that time and shows how dramatically different our society views the teen years now as opposed to fifty years ago. Indeed, before the latter half of the twentieth century, marrying and starting a family in the teen years was the norm, not the exception. Biologically, people in their teen years are *supposed* to be interested in finding a mate: their raging hormones make it painfully important to them. Hormones control their thoughts, their bodies, their entire being at this time, yet the public school system wants them to memorize thousands of irrelevant details, sit still for hours every day, and fight their biological urges at all times. Our society has, in effect, through the school system and other social programs, sought to artificially extend childhood, even though doing so is at odds with nature. People should realize by now that any attempt to manipulate nature usually backfires, and the current non-marital teen pregnancy rate is a prime example of this.

Many people believe that teens don't make good parents, but the fact is that throughout most of human history, people became parents in their teen years and they were good parents. Think about your own parents and grandparents. Chances are they started their families in their teens. The only difference between the good teen parents of yesteryear and the irresponsible, immature teen parents of today is in the education, preparation, and example for parenting (or lack thereof) that they received from their own parents.

I am certainly not advocating that we encourage teens to have sex or to marry at a young age, but rather, that we offer a system of education where students learn to be responsible for their own lives, where they can finish their education early, if they so choose, and begin their adult lives prepared to succeed; where they can choose to start a family because they are ready and prepared to take on that responsibility, not because they are rebelling against the system or just plain being irresponsible.

Substance Abuse

The rising rate of teen substance abuse (and, indeed, adult substance abuse, as well) is yet another symptom of a system that encourages dependency and irresponsibility. When teens and adults are faced with the normal problems of life, they are often not equipped with the knowledge and autonomy needed to overcome and deal with them. They often become overwhelmed and turn to drugs or alcohol to escape their problems. Other substance abusers use drugs or alcohol recreationally because they are so used to being entertained extraneously, they cannot amuse themselves any other way. Some substance abusers started out as hyperactive children who were given drugs to calm them down and make them fit into the institution of school.

Many people rely on legal, prescribed mood-altering drugs such as Prozac to help them deal with life. Indeed, Prozac and other, related mood-altering drugs are the fastest growing prescribed drugs in the nation.[9] The problems of today are not worse than they were a hundred years ago; the difference is in the way people choose to deal with them. It is much easier to pop a pill than to face and deal with the problems.

It is imperative that our public school system give students the knowledge and skills needed to deal with life's problems without turning to drugs. Since financial difficulty is a major source of anxiety leading to substance abuse, in-depth education in personal finance is a must. Young adults also need to have the skills to procure and succeed in a job upon graduation in order to have a meaningful career in which to support themselves. Family problems is another leading cause of substance abuse, so family living courses are equally important. Finally, instead of preaching to students about the consequences of substance abuse, which we know often does not work, students must be able to discover the consequences for themselves through research instead of experimentation.

Poor Work Ethic

Many people today claim that Americans are working harder than ever: however, the statistics show otherwise. The average work week for the United States' labor pool in 2001 was 34 hours. By 2008, that figure had dropped to 33.5 hours. Especially troubling is the amount of hours worked by poor families. While non-poor families work, on average, 2,080 hours per year (40 hours per week), poor families averaged barely over half that, or 1,112 hours per year (less than 21.5 hours per week).[10] For the most part, the poor in this country are poor because they don't work as much as the non-poor. Whether this is because of a lack of education, a shortage of job opportunities, problems with arranging for childcare, or just plain laziness, it all stems from not being prepared in school for a working life after graduation.

The United States has entered the age of technology and has left the industrial age behind. That is, except for the public school system. Since our system was set up to prepare students for working in factories during the industrial age, it is not surprising that they are not prepared for the type of work required in today's technological age. According to a report based on a detailed survey of 431 human resource officials in 2006, high school graduates entering the work force lack the basic skills of reading comprehension, writing, and math, combined with deficiencies in "applied" skills such as professionalism and work ethic (defined as demonstrating personal accountability, punctuality, working productively with others, time and workload management, etc.). Some of the greatest deficiencies cited were in basic English writing skills, such as grammar and spelling, critical thinking, and creativity. Survey participants also noted several key skills projected to increase in importance for future graduates: making appropriate choices concerning health and wellness (such as making healthy food choices, exercise, and stress reduction), creativity/innovation, and knowledge of foreign languages and cultures.[11]

Our school system's main goal should be to prepare students for a successful and productive future. This is not only good for each individual student, but imperative for the success of our nation, as well. One of the most important facets of this preparedness is the education and tools needed to succeed in the kinds of jobs that will be available to them when they graduate. We must realize that the industrial age is over and begin to train our students for work in business, technology, and service areas rather than training them to be factory workers. Obviously, from the results of the survey described above and many others as well, two of the most important aspects of job training are communication skills and work ethic, both of which the current system is failing to teach adequately.

Obesity

Why are so many Americans obese? The answer is that we are not taught two things: healthy habits and self-control. In our present culture, children are supposed to learn about healthy habits from their parents. Somewhere along the line, in the past fifty years or so, many parents stopped modeling behaviors like this. Instead, they started teaching unhealthy habits by example. People stopped being active, started becoming "couch potatoes," eating fried and processed foods, wanting more and more, and not exercising self control in eating. We became a very over-indulgent culture. What we want, we want immediately, and we get it. We want our food fast, easy, and in unlimited supply. MacDonald's is not to blame for our "super-size me" culture: it is the citizens who demand it. This is what our children have learned, and it is no wonder that the outlook for the future of our children's health is bleak. Even though the system feels it should be in the restaurant business (feeding breakfast and lunch to students), it does not take advantage of the teaching moment every day as it feeds all these children. Often, schools feed unhealthy food to the students: fried and processed foods, sweets, even soda. Students eat in a large cafeteria, the only adult there being an authority figure who constantly yells to keep control. It seems the system is at least partly responsible for the declining health of the country. At the very least, it is not helping the problem.

The system needs to not only get out of the restaurant business, but also to educate students about staying healthy. I know that most schools (at least elementary schools) *preach* healthy habits, but it is not *taught* by example. When children are told to eat right and stay active, yet the institution telling them this expects them to sit still all day and serves them unhealthy food for lunch, and even many of the teachers themselves lead unhealthy lives, children will not listen; as with many other hollow lessons it "goes in one ear and out the other."

Instead, schools should not only teach healthy habits, but practice them as well. The Japanese have great success with whole school exercise programs such as Tai Chi before school starts and at intervals throughout the day. Lessons can be taught on how to prepare healthy lunches and children can be encouraged to make their own healthy lunches at home to bring to school. Teachers should eat with their students in the classroom where healthy and enjoyable discussion can take place, instead of the institutional lunchroom where chaos rules. After lunch, cleaning up after oneself should be an unquestioned routine. A brief after-lunch break would help recharge students' (and teachers') brains. This break could be simply free time to socialize in the classroom or outside, or time to lay down your head and take a little nap, if desired. When the break is over, another round of group exercise will rev up the brain and body again for school work. In other words, exercise and healthy eating are treated as a way of life, a routine, not as a subject or a class to go to twice a week and have to be tested on.

Lack of Creativity, Imagination, and Spontaneity

Most of the activity of children today is directed by adults, both at school and at home. Children's thoughts are controlled by school teachers, parents, and media. They are told what to learn, what to think, how to act, and even how to play. What used to be just a doll is now "Dora," "Barbie," or "Bratz," each packaged with its own video to give ideas on how to play with them. What used to be just a train set is now "Thomas the Tank Engine," with books and videos to provide stories to direct play. The mass marketing of "play" is huge business now, but the result is children who cannot think creatively for themselves. Boys used to play sandlot baseball or impromptu games of football in the backyard with few props; now they must be enrolled in adult-controlled leagues with expensive equipment and fenced-in fields. Even playgrounds have become more and more adult-directed in nature. The asphalt is painted with four-square and basketball courts; play equipment now comes with built-in activities, such as tic-tac-toe boards and pre-fabricated cottages. Agatha Christie said it eloquently:

> "I suppose it is because nearly all children go to school nowadays and have things arranged for them that they seem so forlornly unable to produce their own ideas."

There has been a grassroots movement toward more old-fashioned, imagination-provoking toys in recent years, but too many children today are wrapped up in cartoons and video games to make these kinds of toys popular. The parents who choose these simple toys for their children correctly sense that the simplicity of them will encourage creativity and imagination. Unfortunately, too many parents buy into the media hype and false-hero worship (like the "Hannah Montana" craze) when choosing toys for their children, setting the stage for a life of needing to be extraneously entertained.

The dearth of creativity and imagination among the young people of the United States is a direct result of too much control over their lives. As soon as children enter school, they are expected to relinquish their minds to the control of adults. They are not expected to think for themselves, only to "soak up" the words of their teacher as she or he lectures at the front of the class. Problem solving and critical thinking are not an important part of the school day. Many times, an original, correct answer will be counted wrong because it is not the answer the teacher was looking for. After twelve or thirteen years of being encouraged to not think for themselves, children lose this skill along with its companion skills – creativity, imagination, and spontaneity. They become passive. This passivity, which is now called "learned helplessness," is the students' response to external control of their environment. This learned helplessness does not disappear when students graduate from high school. It continues throughout life and manifests itself in many of the problems covered in this section such as substance abuse, irresponsibility, and obesity.

The public school system should be a place where imagination and creativity are not only encouraged, but necessary to earn an education. What other place is more suited to be an incubator for ideas and innovations of the future?

Lack of Common Sense

The United States has become a country almost devoid of common sense. Our laws, our courts, our various governmental entities, and especially our public school system have been designed to prevent people from using common sense. The blanket "one-size-fits-all" treatment of problems and everyday governmental transactions has frustrated and angered citizens for years, yet most people don't question the fact that the use of common sense is almost non-existent in the way schools are run, especially with zero-tolerance policies.

There are many examples of this fact. Most of us have heard about the kindergarten boy who was expelled for kissing girls on the playground – sexual harassment in the eyes of public school law. Or how about a third grader suspended for bringing a tiny plastic toy gun to school – weapons violation. Or the three kindergartners suspended for playing "cops and robbers" on the playground. If educated school officials can't be trusted to use common sense in individual cases, than what hope do we have of our children growing up learning to use common sense?

We don't have hope as it is now. We know that many of our citizens are making choices in their lives without using a shred of common sense. Our courts are filled with lawsuits against manufacturers for injuries sustained by the plaintiff after making bad choices while using the defendant's product. Our roads have become even more dangerous with people choosing to text while driving. Our prisons are overflowing with people who are not inherently criminals but who have simply made bad choices in their lives. The examples and the effects of the lack of common sense are everywhere.

We need to be able to rely on our system of public education to encourage our young people to develop common sense and to use that common sense when making choices in their lives. Our current system punishes bad choices but does not give students the tools to understand their choices and to make good ones. The use of common sense should be nurtured and rewarded in our schools but, instead, it is sacrificed for the sake of conformity and obedience.

Ignorance of Government and Laws

The lack of understanding of how government works in this country is appalling and embarrassing. The many facets of our country's government (including local, state, and national) are complex and fascinating. The rudiments of our national government are usually taught in elementary school but the concepts are too abstract for young children to comprehend and internalize. In high school, students are usually required to take only one course in United States government (either a semester or two semester course). It is impossible to fully understand and remember all the components by taking a semester or even a year of government class.

I am a college-educated person, yet I do not know all the laws and regulations of this land. So many times we hear of people in court using the defense, "I didn't know I was breaking the law," to no avail since "ignorance of the law is no excuse." Yet, think about it: where and how are we supposed to learn laws? The school system doesn't teach them effectively. If our parents don't know all the laws, they can't teach us, and we can't teach them to our children. I don't even know where a person could go to read about all the laws, rules, and regulations in this nation. The library? The courthouse? The Internet?

The school system is responsible for the education of our citizens. Education about the laws and regulations of this country should be required in school, as well as more than one semester of government class. It is said that most native-born U.S. citizens could not pass the test for citizenship. That is a pitiful testimonial about the quality of education citizens in this country receive. It is quite embarrassing that an immigrant is more knowledgeable about our government when becoming a citizen than natural-born citizens are. The ability to pass the citizenship test should be required of any graduate of the system.

Vehicle Deaths

Many deaths and injuries in automobiles are caused by drivers' lack of skill, poor judgment, inattention, and not realizing the significance and consequences of all these things. Driving is a skill that is so important to the safety and welfare of the population, it should be taught in the school system, yet most people dismiss it as not being important to teach. Over eight times more people die *each year* on our nation's highway than the total of U.S. casualties in the wars in Afghanistan and Iraq in the last eight years combined.[12] People of this country are distraught by the casualties of the wars in the Middle East, but think nothing of the vehicle deaths. Even though war casualties are very unfortunate, at least the soldiers are dying for a cause that they are getting paid to defend, instead of the totally senseless deaths of innocent men, women, and children on our highways. Over 40% more of our citizens die on our roads and highways than are killed by guns each year[13], yet we don't hear of organizations trying to take motor vehicles away from people to stop the senseless killing.

I realize that implementing a drivers' education program that involves vehicles, instructors, and insurance is very expensive, which is why most public schools don't do it anymore, but by freeing money up that is spent on feeding students, for example, it can and should be done. Even if the instruction is merely class-based and not vehicular-based (i.e., no actual driving), it would be helpful in increasing student's knowledge of laws, safety, defensive driving, consequences, etc. Also, there are many vehicle driving simulators on the market which could come close to the real thing. With the inordinate number of vehicle deaths, many of them young people, teaching vehicular safety is an extremely important obligation of the public school system, not an optional course.

Hyperactivity

In the old days (i.e. the days before mandatory public schooling), a person with high levels of energy (now called hyperactivity) was able to channel that energy into success at farming, ranching, business, whatever enterprise he or she was interested in. It is only because of the institutional setting of the public school system that we now feel that something must be wrong with these high-energy children, something that needs to be medicated and squashed. It is no wonder that these children often become discipline problems, and, later on in life, some become criminals and drug addicts. It is not the children who need to be fixed; it is the system that needs fixing. At no other time in a person's life is he or she required to sit still and be quiet for six or seven hours a day. Some careers may require it, but people are not forced into those careers, and usually, high-energy people will not choose those careers. We are wasting the potential of these young people by stifling them and trying to eliminate their high-energy, making them into angry, self-loathing adults who think they are flawed. Instead, we should be channeling all this energy in creative and productive ways so they grow into energetic adults with a thirst for success. This is nearly impossible in the current system of education.

According to the National Institutes of Health, attention-deficit/hyperactivity disorder (ADHD) affects only 3-5% of the population, yet nearly half of school-age boys in this country are now diagnosed with the disorder and prescribed psychoactive drugs to make them more manageable in a classroom setting. As Peg Tyre, a Pulitzer Prize-winning author, says in her book The Trouble With Boys,

> *"That such large numbers of boys are being diagnosed with a central nervous system disorder suggests two things: Either we are witnessing the largest pandemic in our country since influenza struck the United States in 1918, or school-age boys are being overidentified and overdiagnosed."* [14]

In The Myth of the Hyperactive Child, Peter Schrag and Diane Divoky contend that

> *"[a] small percentage of those children [taking amphetamine-type drugs and other psychostimulants] suffer from some diagnosable medical ailment sufficiently serious to warrant chemotherapy. Most do not; they are being drugged at the insistence of schools or individual teachers, to make them more manageable."* [15]

Even as early as in 1862, Leo Tolstoy realized that

> *"[c]hildren's conversation, motion, and merriment [in school] ... are not convenient for the teacher, and so in the schools, which*

are built on the plan of prisons, questions, conversation, and motion are prohibited."

Many so-called hyperactive students are also highly intelligent and get bored with the slower paced learning of the "normal" students. They need to move ahead, be challenged, to work at their own pace. Many hyperactive students have one or more learning disabilities (which are not an indication of intelligence) that cause them to lag behind in one or more subjects. The snowball effect of missing vital building blocks in those subjects cause self esteem problems that, in turn, cause the student to give up on learning and on themselves.

In effect, what the system is doing is trying to make all children, with all their ranges of human behavior, fit into a narrow definition of what is "normal" and desirable for the institution of public school. Figuratively, they are changing the various shapes of children, which may include ovals, squares, triangles, and even polyhedrons, to fit into a perfectly round slot. In order to do this, the system must resort to subjecting children to behavior modification and drugs. Instead of changing the shape of the system, the system chooses to modify the shape of millions of children, with little or no thought to the long-term effects of these strategies on the children they are forced upon. According to Schrag and Divoky,

> *"millions of children are no longer regarded as part of the ordinary spectrum of human personality and intelligence—children who are quieter or brighter than the average, children who are jumpy, children who are slow—but as people who are qualitatively different from the 'normal' population, individuals who, as a consequence of 'minimal brain dysfunction,' 'hyperactivity,'*

or 'functional behavior disorders,' constitute a distinct and separate group." [16]

Our school system needs to be a system that provides a flexible opening (as opposed to a perfectly round one), which can change to accommodate the shape of each student without having to modify the student with drugs or psychotherapy; where students can work at their own pace in each subject, never having to worry about where the rest of the class is; where teachers can modify and personalize the lessons to teach to the learning abilities and disabilities of a student and give one-on-one attention when needed; where students can excel in the areas they are naturally good in, giving them a shot of well-earned self esteem, while getting the help they need to succeed in the other subjects as well; where high energy can be encouraged and nurtured through alternative methods of learning instead of being suppressed.

Financial Woes

Financial crises, home mortgage crises, crushing credit card debt, social security shortfalls. These are problems you hear about in the news everyday. All are preventable, if only students were taught personal finance. Not one semester of it in high school, but throughout their entire school careers. Personal finance can and should be taught from the earliest grades continuously until graduation. Understanding how to manage one's own personal finances, instead of entrusting that job to the government or financial institutions, is the most efficient and effective way of solving most of the financial woes people will be confronted with in the future.

As I write this, the government has just signed a $700 billion bill to bail out failing financial institutions in order to get our economy on solid ground again. What caused these failures in the first place? Greed, of course, is probably the biggest contributor, but greed can only gain footing if there are people who allow, through ignorance, the greedy to take advantage of them. Individuals who were directly hurt, for example, by the home mortgage crisis of 2008, when mortgage companies such as Fannie Mae and Freddie Mac loaned billions of dollars to people who could not afford to pay back their mortgages, trusted the financial institution blindly. They unknowingly put their financial futures in jeopardy. There's no good reason why these people and all others educated in the public school system could not have been taught about mortgages, interest rates, compound interest, etc., so they could have made informed decisions about such an important part of modern life. It's certainly more important to real life than knowing trigonometry.

There is a lot of talk about how the Social Security System will be bankrupt in a few years. If that happens, all the money that working people today are forced by the federal government to pay into the Social Security Administration will be lost, leaving them destitute in their retirement years, unless they are wise enough to save for themselves. Most United States citizens won't save enough, though. The U.S. Department of Labor estimates that one-third of American workers do not save for retirement and more than half of the two-thirds who do have a retirement savings account have saved woefully inadequate amounts.[17]

Instead of saving, we spend. We live in a society of manic consumers. The United States is the largest consumer economy on Earth. We have to have the newest gadgets, the latest trends, large collections of useless things. There are now almost 18% more passenger vehicles owned in the United States than there are drivers.[18] Many people boast of their massive shoe collection (both men and women), their extravagant $300 purse, their acquisition of the latest games and gaming systems. Almost every household in the United States, no matter the household income, has at least one television. The early industrialists who poured money into the public school system would be very pleased with the nation of consumers they created – citizens who must consume to feel validated and to experience personal happiness.

Where does this mania to spend and ignorance of financial matters come from? From a system that encourages dependency and irresponsibility instead of giving students the tools they need to survive in the world. The school system must refocus its energy to educate and encourage financial responsibility and independence. This cannot be done in a semester class of personal finance. It must be taught from the earliest school years and continued throughout a student's school career. Personal finance should be as elemental to the school curricula as is English or mathematics. In fact, it should be taught as a real-life application of mathematics, serving the dual purposes of teaching personal finance and reinforcing the mathematical concepts used in finance (counting money, balancing a checkbook, figuring out how much needs to be saved for a future purchase, making a budget, figuring out the true cost of borrowing money, etc.)

Stop Beating the Dead Horse

The great social problems facing our citizens today are not unavoidable catastrophes – they are all preventable with the right education. As citizens paying taxes for a public school system, we have the right to receive an education that will protect us from these problems and ensure our unalienable rights of life, liberty, and the pursuit of happiness. We have allowed the public school system to usurp and undercut our rights – as parents and as citizens – long enough. It is time to demand that our public education system meet the needs of our citizens in an effective and productive manner. It is time to dismount the dead horse and find a new one which will address the fundamental problems with the current system and provide the education we, as tax-paying citizens, deserve.

Three

The Fundamental Problems With the Current System

(The Same Old Horse)

I have identified seven fundamental problems that I believe are the main areas that need to be addressed and changed for a new system to work in today's world.

Problem #1 Dividing students by age: Students are expected to be at the *same level* in each subject as every other student who is the *same chronological age.*

When children are in the infant and toddler stages of life, child experts are adamant that each child is unique and will reach milestones in his or her own timeframe. Yet, when a child turns five, he or she must begin performing milestones, such as learning to read and write, to add and subtract, get along with peers, etc., at the same time as every other child his or her age, regardless of individual biorhythms or past experiences and preparation; else risk attaining only partial mastery of the milestone or even failing to reach it altogether. These failures to master concepts start snowballing as the child continues in school, causing low self-esteem and failure in others areas of life. Sometimes a failing student can recover if the time is right for them to learn a specific task and she or he has not missed too many concepts along the way, but many failing students continue to fail or to just barely pass the rest of their school career – all because they were forced to learn something they weren't quite ready to understand yet. Why do our schools employ a system that is contrary to what child experts preach? Because it has been done that way for a hundred years or so and few have thought to change it.

Peg Tyre, in <u>The Trouble With Boys</u>, describes why many boys (and probably some girls, as well) have trouble in school—their first experiences in school come at a time when their bodies aren't capable of doing what is asked of them. She writes,

> *"...when you send your son off to preschool, he may repeatedly experience things that he finds frustrating, uncomfortable, or alienating. He may encounter expectations that are so at odds with his natural development that they leave him bewildered and angry. His preschool experience may plant in him the seed of a bitter weed, which may grow into the conviction that formal education is simply not for him. Instead of fostering a love of learning, his days in preschool may shake his confidence to the core."* [1]

The converse of this problem consists of the students who are well advanced of their peers. Although they may appear to do better in school, the constant restraining of their intelligence to keep them in line with the other students of their same chronological age will often eventually lead to a lack of interest in learning and suppression of their natural curiosity. C. S. Lewis, British novelist of the early 20th century, described public schooling in this way:

> *"The basic proposal of the new education is to be that dunces and idlers must not be made to feel inferior to intelligent and industrious pupils. That would be 'undemocratic.' Children who are fit to proceed may be artificially kept back, because the others would get a trauma by being left behind. The bright pupil thus remains democratically fettered to his own age group throughout his school career, and a boy who would be capable of tackling Aeschylus or Dante sits listening to his coeval's attempts to spell out A CAT SAT ON A MAT...All incentives to learn and all penalties for not learning will vanish. The few who might want to learn will be prevented; who are they to overtop their fellows? And anyway, the teachers -- or should I say nurses? -- will be far too busy reassuring the dunces and patting them on the back to waste any time on real teaching. We shall no longer have to plan and toil to spread imperturbable conceit and incurable ignorance among men."*

In our quest to make every child equal (homogenous), we must use the least common denominator (i.e. the lowest performing student), thereby "dumbing down" the entire country. Al McGuire wittily remarked, *"I think the world is run by C students."* We need a system of education in which every student can perform to his/her own abilities and not be held back or forced ahead to stay even with all the other students the same age. If we are truly a culture born of diversity and one that embraces those differences, then why does our school system expect everyone of the same age to be exactly the same academically?

Problem #2 Focusing on details: Students are expected to learn *too much detail* on each subject so that not enough time is spent mastering the basic concepts that all other learning is based on.

Much school time is spent, for example, on learning how to diagram sentences (a skill that is unnecessary to adult life – how many adults can tell what a past participle is and how it is used in a sentence?), while students (and adults) continue to speak incorrect English and cannot communicate effectively, either written or orally. Students in high school must learn geometry and trigonometry, while, at the same time, many cannot count back change at the checkout, balance a checkbook, or figure a 15% tip on a restaurant bill. Students are also forced to memorize thousands of dates in history but cannot explain what the War of 1812 was about (if they remember it at all). Especially at the high school level, information is fed to students that most adults do not need to know to thrive in society, yet many experts think that the reason our students don't test well compared to those in other countries is that we need to feed them more details. I say the opposite is true: the details are quickly forgotten because they are not important to remember. Unfortunately, the fundamentals are also forgotten because, in the quest for more detail, we do not have enough time to reinforce the basics. Therefore, students cannot answer even the basic questions they need to be successful. Henry Brooks Adams, Pulitzer prize-winning historian, and great-grandson of John Adams stated,

Stop Beating the Dead Horse

> *"Nothing in education is so astonishing as the amount of ignorance it accumulates in the form of inert facts."*

Recent brain research has shown that during adolescence, children go through a period of brain development in which neurons are pruned. Apparently, the pruning happens on a "use-it-or-lose-it" basis. Information that was taught in elementary school may get pruned along with the myriad of facts memorized in junior high and high school which are useful only for passing the test at the end of the chapter. Only that information which is used often in the adolescent's life will be retained. A few years ago, my husband, a junior high and high school science teacher in the public school system, told me about a study done in which junior high school students were asked to recite times tables and name the months of the year in order. Most of the students in the study, as well as my husband's junior high students, failed to remember these elementary facts. I remember thinking that my son, who was twelve at the time and homeschooled, surely could do better. I was wrong. It made me rethink what was important to teach him during his teen years. Much of his junior high and high school work was focused on relearning and reinforcing basic skills and learning to think for himself. He is now doing quite well in college, despite never having taken many of the courses required in a public high school curriculum.

Robert Hutchins, educational philosopher and dean of Yale Law School (1927-1929) said,

> *"It must be remembered that the purpose of education is not to fill the minds of students with facts... it is to teach them to think, if that is possible, and always to think for themselves.*

Diane Ravitch, former U.S. assistant secretary of Education, reports that 78 percent of colleges in the United States offer remedial courses in reading, writing, and math, and that *"it is fairly shocking, or should be, to discover that 29 percent of all freshman take a remedial course when they enter college."* [2] That nearly one-third of college-bound students need remedial help in core subjects is direct proof of the failure of the public education system to teach the basics in a way that ensures mastery of these subjects.

We need a system of education that continually reinforces the basics, ensuring that a permanent foundation will be formed in the brains of students and allowing for the addition of as many details as each student desires to learn.

Problem #3 Lack of relevance: Many of the things taught in the public school system are *irrelevant* to most people's lives, whereas many of the things that are relevant to virtually everyone's lives are barely, or not at all, taught.

It is a well known fact that optimum learning is achieved when the subject is relevant to the learner. Irrelevance leads to boredom and sometimes anger, especially in teenagers. Making subjects relative to students' lives will not only greatly enhance learning, but will also lessen the problems associated with bored and angry students. For example, teaching physics to 10th graders (most of whom are 15 to 16 years old) will probably not interest many of them, but if the teacher ties the physics concepts to driving a car, most students at this age will be interested, especially if the lessons are presented as a way to make students better drivers. The benefits of this method are twofold: students are more receptive to the physics concepts and they become better drivers. Better drivers, in turn, mean fewer traffic deaths. Everything taught in schools should be with the goal of making adult life easier and more productive. The mortgage crisis of 2008 could have been averted if students had been taught personal finance all through their school careers. Biology classes spend a lot of time learning the stages of cell division, but, apparently, not enough time learning what happens when one has unprotected sex. Students are graduating high school without knowing that their boyfriend/girlfriend is not supposed to beat up on them, or that they have to hold and take care of a baby, let alone how to manage a household, write a coherent letter, or build good credit. These things may be taught in high schools, but too often, they are not required or are only semester courses without enough repetition to enforce retention.

We need a system of education in which only those things that are relevant to living in the world today are required and non-relevant subjects are elective. We need a system that ensures a better quality of life for our students when they reach adulthood and also a better informed citizenry.

Problem #4 Grading and testing: Grades and tests are given as the *end product of a lesson* instead of as a means to the more important end – *mastery of the lesson.*

There is little or no time to go back and remediate for students who have not mastered a lesson before moving on to the next lesson: therefore, a student who makes anything below 100% may miss vital building blocks to the next lesson. Those students making below a "C" also risk damage to their self-esteem by being labeled, by the grade itself, as below average or a failure. Standardized achievement tests cause further damage to a struggling student by comparing him or her to other students, yet little or no remediation is offered for the student since the results often aren't received until the following school year. Parenting experts are adamant that parents not compare their children to other children to avoid risking permanent damage to their self esteem, yet this is done every day in the current public school system by assigning letter grades. Any grade below 100% means that mastery of the lesson has not occurred.

Assigning letter grades serves no real purpose, when you think about it. A student making all "A's" gets the exact same instruction as a student making all "D's"; they receive an identical diploma when they graduate. The grade does not always reflect a student's intelligence or ability, but rather his or her effort and willingness to perform the tasks assigned by the teacher. Some very intelligent and capable students are given failing or near failing grades because they simply don't want to complete busy work and irrelevant tasks, while other, less intellectually talented students, graduate with honors because they are willing to perform. Anna Quindlen, Pulitzer Prize-winning columnist and author, wrote,

> *"Students absorb the message that learning is a joyless succession of hoops through which they must jump, rather than a way of understanding and mastering the world."*

Sometimes, teachers and administrators feel that they are forced to inflate grades in order to elevate students' self esteem, pacify parents, or meet standards of academic success. This grade inflation serves only to give a false impression of our students' academic progress and to mask the failure of the system. According to Martin L. Gross,

> *"Since the schools are being attacked by critics armed with strong evidence from the states, Washington, and international competition that they are* not *doing a good job educating the young, why not simply outflank the opposition by producing legions of 'honor students'?"*[3]

Grade inflation is just another proof that grades are irrelevant in education and need to be disposed of.

We need a system of education that acknowledges and rewards effort *and* ability, a system that clearly shows the level each student has obtained and mastered by graduation so that future employers know what they are getting. It also must be a system that does not focus on grading and testing as a means to categorize and demean students, but rather, only as a means to show mastery of concepts.

Problem #5 Lack of freedom to learn: Students are not given the freedom to explore things that interest them, thereby *missing out on valuable learning and the intrinsic motivation to learn.*

William Butler Yeats, Nobel Laureate in Literature of the late 19th and early 20th centuries, noted,

> *"Education is not the filling of a pail, but the lighting of a fire."*

Ralph Waldo Emerson noted,

> *"Scholarship is to be created not by compulsion, but by awakening a pure interest in knowledge."*

Robert Maynard Hutchins, educational philosopher, dean of Yale Law School, and president of the University of Chicago, said,

> *"The objective of education is to prepare the young to educate themselves throughout their lives."*

George Bernard Shaw remarked,

> *"What we want is to see the child in pursuit of knowledge, and not knowledge in pursuit of the child."*

What did all these learned men know that the current school system misses? They knew that children need the freedom to learn things that interest them; that they need to be given the opportunity to develop their own optimum methods of learning, encouraged to find their own inspiration, and authorized to discover as much as they want. We need a system of education that allows all this to happen so that we will have generations of citizens who can think and do for themselves, who will never lose their zest for learning, and who can lead this country back to the forefront of technology and democracy.

Problem #6 Lack of student responsibility: Students have *no responsibility* for their own education.

Just as a person often does not take good care of something that is given to him/her, so it is with education. Students must have an internal motivation and be held responsible for their education. They must feel like they need to *earn* their education and that it is something vital to being able to grow up and live on their own. Too many times in our public school system, students are being passed to the next grade with little or no comprehension of the information in the previous grade and even less effort by the student to learn. This leads students to believe they don't have to try in order to get by. As mentioned before (and it bears repeating), students who graduate with barely passing grades get exactly the same diploma as those who achieved all "A's". Many students feel that education is something done *to* them, forced upon them, something they neither want nor need. They don't take responsibility for their education, nor do they see the benefit to themselves. Many students in this country also have a sense of entitlement; they believe that education should be served to them on a platter and that they can pick and choose what to partake of, if anything. Then they expect, as adults, to have a high paying job or have the government take care of them. After all, that is how they were raised by the system to think. So much time and money is spent trying to make better qualified and more accountable teachers, but the problem is **not** the teachers. The problem is a system that does not hold *students* accountable for their education.

Abigail Adams said,

> *"Learning is not attained by chance, it must be sought for with ardor and attended to with diligence."*

Many school districts are now trying desperately to improve students' test scores by making the teachers directly accountable for the students' performance. Teachers can face unsatisfactory reviews, lowered salaries, and even be fired based on their students' standardized test scores. This is just another bandage, and a poor one at that, to try to fix the badly bleeding system. It will never work because the *students don't care*: they don't care about their own test scores, they don't care about the country's ranking among other nations, and they don't care about their teachers' careers. They feel no responsibility whatsoever for their own education. I remember asking my son and a bunch of his friends how they did on the standardized test at the end of one school year. They all replied that they didn't even read the questions; they just darkened circles at random. When I asked them why they did this, they answered that it didn't matter at all to their grades, so why should they try? Now, in some districts, a teacher could lose his or her job over this pervasive student attitude of carelessness.

We need a system of education in which each student is responsible for his or her own education, a system that allows students to decide the kind of future employment that interests them and to be able to prepare themselves for that future.

Problem #7 Lack of flexibility in the system: Most importantly, the current public school system makes it very difficult to *implement real change* in order to make the system fit today's needs.

Many pseudo changes are implemented in schools without any real change in the outcome. Just as the dead horse parable in Chapter 1 illustrates, implementing these pseudo changes really doesn't change the fact that the horse (and the system of public education) is dead. Educators do everything in their power, often passionately, to make the system work, but they still must work within the confines of that system and, therefore, cannot make any real difference on a national scale.

We need a system that has the flexibility to allow for not only individual changes at the student level, but also within the entire system itself. As we have seen in the history of the United States public school system, what worked then does not work now, and what works now may not work in the future. We need to be able to make real changes to the system to be able to keep up with the phenomenal rate of change going on in the world today.

~

Of course, there are many other problems associated with the public school system. The practice of making classes teacher-centric and relying on lecture is proven to be an inefficient method of transmitting information. In his book <u>Chalkbored: What's Wrong with School and How to Fix It</u>, Jeremy Schneider rates the reliance on lecture as *"the most glaring example of the problems plaguing education."*[4] Schneider backs up this statement with scientific studies that dramatically show how inefficient and inadequate lecturing (accompanied by its partner – note-taking) is. Like me, Schneider believes the underlying foundation of our educational system is flawed. He writes,

> *"If educators had a slogan, it would be "Teaching the three R's," representing the first three letters of "reading, 'riting, and 'rithmetic" or "reading, writing, and arithmetic" – ironically broadcasting that we either cannot spell or cannot add. Our inability to get even the basics right exposes our real problem. Modern education fails because it is built on an unstable foundation – the principles and pillars that support it are inherently flawed and crumbling.*

> *Unfortunately, the crisis is not so superficial that it can be patched with a new slogan, a better PR firm, or a mountain of educational jargon intended to rename and disguise old issues.*"[5]

Schneider, who is a high school chemistry teacher, goes on to say,

> *"Adults easily forget how bad school is because they have been removed from it for so long. It really is insufferable...The magnitude of this unnecessary misery is a crime that has few parallels."*[6]

George Bernard Shaw also felt that way about school. He wrote,

> *"There is, on the whole, nothing on earth intended for innocent people so horrible as a school."*

It is vital to the future of our country that we replace the current, flawed system of education with something new that will educate our citizens to live and prosper in the world today. In the next section, I will propose a new system (a proverbial new horse), which addresses all the previously mentioned concerns, drawing on ideas from several other sources and from examples of systems already in place and working in this country.

Stop Beating the Dead Horse

SECTION 2: SOLUTIONS
A New Horse!

Stop Beating the Dead Horse 68

Four

The Level Mastery System
(A Horse of a Different Color)

> *"If we value independence, if we are disturbed by the growing conformity of knowledge, of values, of attitudes, which our present system induces, then we may wish to set up conditions of learning which make for uniqueness, for self-direction, and for self-initiated learning."* Carl Rogers.

The Level Mastery System is an idea that evolved over several years of discussion between my husband and me. It is a system that completely changes the way we think of public education and seeks to address the problems put forth in the previous chapters. In order to fully understand and embrace this system, we must first erase all the preconceived notions of what public schooling is. The presuppositions that public schools must be run like prisons, that children must learn each task at exactly the same time and in the same manner, that public schooling should replace parental control and responsibilities, and that students need to be institutionalized and given identical educations, must be expunged from our collective minds. The Level Mastery System would completely replace the current system; it would throw out the proverbial "dead horse" and replace it with a new dynamic one that can, in turn, be replaced as needed *before* it dies. Only in this way can the system be turned around and made viable for educating students in the 21st century and beyond.

When I started writing this book, my research revealed that my ideas (much to my surprise) were not entirely novel and unique. There are numerous educators who have come to many of the same conclusions I have about the system and several who have similar ideas of how to change it. This further reinforces my belief that the time has come to take the plunge – it is time for all the skeptics and the people who are afraid to make a real change to leave the dead horse where it lies and embrace a new one.

Instead of a liberal arts curriculum for the Basic Diploma, I propose a system based on learning practical skills. A liberal arts curriculum usually consists of classes in literature, languages, philosophy, history, mathematics, and science. While each of these subjects is beneficial for many students to learn, *every one* may not be valuable for *every* student. In this century, education must be focused on those skills that most people need to know in order to live a happy, healthy, and successful life. Many of these skills are part of a liberal arts education and are taught in the current system; however, there are also many that are ignored. For example, skills such as written and oral communication and basic mathematics are now taught (although apparently, not very effectively), but geography and personal finance are neglected. Many of the skills and subjects required in the current system are completely extraneous to the lives of the majority of citizens. Many educators believe that it is beneficial to learn these irrelevant facts in order to make a more well-rounded student, but the reality is that students do not retain these facts, making the hours spent teaching and learning them seem like busy-work meant only to fill time. How many adults, besides educators who teach these facts to students or experts working in that particular field, remember (or even care about) things such as how to figure the volume of a box, or the phases of mitosis, or exactly what the three witches prophesied in the Shakespeare play Macbeth? Yet, how many adults would not benefit from knowing how to manage their money, understanding the location and culture of Afghanistan, or knowing what food to eat in order to maintain a healthy weight? In the past, these things were not important or even applicable to life, but today they are critical. The Basic Diploma should consist of the mastery of certain skills to become a happy and productive member of society, not merely a conglomeration of facts and details that do not apply to everyday life. The justification for teaching a liberal arts curriculum to everyone no longer applies to life today. It is time to change the way we evaluate what to teach our students and how they are taught.

This is not to say, however, that a student who is interested in a traditional liberal arts education should be prevented from pursuing that course. In the Level Mastery System, students would be free to pursue knowledge in whatever subjects interest them. No appropriate subject would be off limits. Students would be *required* to master specific skills needed to earn a Basic or Advanced Diploma, but not limited to learning only those skills. Furthermore, some Advanced Diplomas (which are explained in more detail in Chapter 8), particularly some of the college preparatory ones, will require more of a liberal arts curriculum simply to pass college entrance exams and to do well in college.

The basis for the Level Mastery System is the opportunity for individualized learning for each student and the responsibility for that learning to belong to the student. Whole group instruction would be an extracurricular activity instead of the normal way of doing things. Each student would be working independently on a variety of computer and seat work, with occasional small group activities, such as projects and labs. This independent, individualized learning solves many of the problems of the current system, as will be explained in the next chapter, and ensures that each student gets the education he/she needs and desires. As Isaac Asimov, 20th century American author and professor of biochemistry, said,

> *"Self-education is, I firmly believe, the only kind of education there is."*

The idea of individualized mastery learning has actually been around in America for at least 90 years, most notably with the Winnetka Plan in 1919, so named for the school district in which it was implemented. This plan, an experiment in non-graded, individualized learning, emphasized quality of learning rather than time spent learning. According to Winnetka's superintendent at the time,

> *"The underlying philosophy of the Winnetka curriculum was that every normal child master the knowledges and skills he is going to need in life; that every child be given a chance to live happily and richly as a child; that every child be given an opportunity to develop fully his own individuality; and that all children be brought to the fullest possible realization that in the world's good is one's own, and in one's own good is the world's."*
> [1]

The Winnetka Plan was successful in these goals for a decade, but because of the lack of technology to sustain it, interest in the program diminished and education in Winnetka returned to the same old inferior, but familiar and easily-implemented, way of doing things. Since then, there have been numerous attempts to use individualized learning in classrooms and the results of these attempts were promising. Meta-analyses of dozens of studies show that students had increased gains in achievement, retained what they learned longer, and had more positive attitudes toward learning than in traditional instruction programs, and even the teachers were more satisfied with their teaching.[2] But the individualized learning systems of the past were difficult to sustain because the mediums used to implement the individualized learning were tedious, cumbersome, and many times boring. More importantly, the onerous task of implementing these systems ultimately was put on each individual teacher, which was a burden too heavy for most.

Today we have the perfect medium – the computer. There are hundreds, if not thousands, of engaging, edifying, and educationally sound software programs already available (many are even free) to use in implementing a truly individualized mastery learning program. And by having a national framework – a place for a school district to begin when implementing this kind of system – teachers and administrators in each district will not be forced to "reinvent the wheel," so to speak, but instead will be able to personalize the framework to fit the values of the community and the individual students in that district.

In the Level Mastery System, all subjects would be broken down into levels, or natural segments of learning. Each level would have a packet, consisting of the objectives of the level, reading material, computer work, worksheets, craft projects, games, or other fun things to do relating to the subject (all with options for the students to choose what they want to complete – what they believe will help them learn the material – and a final assessment to prove mastery. Classes would consist of 15-30 students of varying ages monitored by a teacher/mentor. In the primary levels, which would focus on acquiring the basic skills to earn the Basic Diploma, one teacher/mentor would provide all the materials and aid for his/her class. Basic concepts would be presented in a variety of ways, targeting all the different styles of learning, so that total mastery of these "building blocks" is achieved.

Students would work on each level at their own pace and would be responsible for seeking help from the teacher and letting the teacher know when they are ready to be assessed. Assessments would be non-threatening, untimed, one-on-one interaction with the teacher/mentor. Assessments would be written and/or oral, depending on the subject and the student's abilities. Only after the student has proved mastery (100% understanding) would he/she be able to move to the next level. A student may be on a different level in each subject, depending on his/her understanding and strengths, e.g. level 20 in reading, but only level 3 in mathematics. The teacher's job would be to put together packets for each student, give help when needed, give assessments, maintain discipline, and provide occasional group activities (challenges that would require the group to solve). Student-to-student tutoring would be encouraged, as this enhances and solidifies understanding for both the tutor and the tutee and fosters an atmosphere of teamwork and mutual respect.

After earning a Basic Diploma, students may choose to continue their education at the secondary level, which would focus on a particular field of study in preparation for an Advanced Diploma. Teacher/mentors at this level would specialize in the subjects of their greatest strengths and education. Students would attend a particular academy (such as The Science and Mathematics Academy or the English and Foreign Languages Academy), depending on their interests, with the ability to change academies if they decide to change their career focus. Students in secondary school (as well as in the elementary level) would have permanent cubicles, much like many offices have, in which to study instead of changing rooms all day long. In this way, they will have continuity in their studies and be more productive in the long run. They will be allowed to take breaks as needed; there will be no bells ringing every fifty minutes. Subjects would be presented as they interrelate to each other and as they are used in the student's intended career path. For example, a student who wishes to pursue a career in the medical field would study the sciences and mathematics, of course, but also Latin and Greek (as much medical terminology is derived from these two languages), communication (both written and oral), and whatever other subjects deemed important and useful by the medical field and helpful to being successful in college. All of the subjects would be presented in relation to the medical field.

Since the focus of the secondary school is preparation for a career, interning at local businesses, preferably in their chosen field of study, if at all possible, would be a part of every Advanced Diploma. The student intern could be paid by the school district at the current minimum wage while working during school hours. This would not only give the student a feeling of being valued, but also allow the student to earn money in direct relation to his or her school work, cutting down the time spent working in the evenings and weekends. A student could choose to participate in several internships during his/her secondary school experience in order to find a career that interests him/her.

A major component of the Level Mastery System would be individual computers for each student. While the expense of this would seem to be relatively high, the benefits far outweigh the cost and there are many possible sources of funding to pursue from businesses and charitable foundations. Hundreds of studies comparing computer-based instruction to traditional classroom instruction consistently show that computers improve test scores, take less time to teach a concept, and improve student attitudes about the lessons.

Computer-based instruction has other benefits, as well. The problem of missing valuable learning time for sick days, snow days, or summer vacation would become a thing of the past. All students would be provided with laptops, making it easy for them to continue their studies at home during vacations or sick days or if they want to pursue an interesting topic after school hours. Imagine a student in the waiting room of a doctor's or dentist's office using the time to further his/her studies. Parents wishing to homeschool their children would be able to use the national framework, as well, giving them a starting point to personalize the program for their families while still ensuring that the basic skills are mastered. Private and parochial schools could also use the framework and modify it to suit their focus, if so desired. Since everyone pays taxes for the education of our students, the resources should be available to all.

Basing instruction on computers also frees up money from other areas, such as textbooks, paper, and writing utensils. Although I'm not advocating replacing all areas of learning with a computer (students still need to learn to write on paper and create works of art, for example), the bulk of paper passed from teacher to student and back to teacher for grading would be greatly reduced and there would be no need for a textbook for each student in each subject.

A computer provides for instant feedback and corrections on many subjects, releasing a teacher from endless hours of grading papers, a task which most teachers dislike. It also frees up a teacher for more individual interaction with students, transforming the image of a teacher from a lecturing disciplinarian to a mentor and an advocate.

Many people are opposed to the use of computers and technology in schools because they envision students playing games and surfing the net instead of learning. Many people were opposed to the printing press and learning from books when they were introduced centuries ago, too. Computer use can be closely monitored so that undesirable activities are blocked. It may sound like computers are in direct contrast to my back-to-the-basics philosophy, but I'd like to point out that the basics I advocate are the skills taught, not the method of instruction. Good educational computer software can teach the basics in a more exciting, engaging way than a lecture can. A computer is merely a tool of the modern age that can be extremely effective when used properly. Knowing how to use computers is vital to future employment, as well, as most jobs – from auto mechanic to zookeeper – use computers in this day and age.

Stop Beating the Dead Horse

Five

How the Level Mastery System Addresses the Fundamental Problems with the Current System

(What to Look for When Buying a New Horse)

This chapter shows how the Level Mastery System addresses the basic problems that are listed in Chapter 3:

Problem #1 Dividing students by age: In the Level Mastery System, students would be doing work at the level immediately above that which they have mastered in each subject *regardless of their chronological age.*

Students would enter the school system when their parents and school officials agree that they are ready mentally, emotionally, and physically. In this way, we can ensure that children are capable of formal education instead of forcing them into a life of frustration and failure. Once they are ready for school, students will begin a journey of individualized and self education, working through each level of each subject at their own pace, truly mastering the material before they move on.

There are schools in the United States that have done away with grade levels with great success. The Chugach School District, based in Anchorage, Alaska, has used a student-centered, standards-based, non-graded approach since 1995 with impressive results.[1] They have been so successful that other school districts are taking notice. At least one district, the Adams 50 School District in Westminster, Colorado – a 10,000 student district in the Metropolitan Denver area – is adopting this radical new approach to learning, as well.[2] After reporting on the Adams 50 School District's undertaking in March of 2009, Parade Magazine reported that a recent poll by parade.com revealed that 77% of respondents believed that schools should end grade levels based on age.[3]

Problem #2 Focusing on details: In the Level Mastery System, high school graduation would require mastery of only the *basic skills* needed to live a productive adult life.

High school graduates need only basic skills to do jobs that hire people with just a high school diploma (e.g. factory workers, bus drivers, store clerks, etc.). Jobs that require advanced schooling, whether technical schools or universities, need the specific skills that are taught in that particular school. Those skills do not need to be taught to every student. For example, a factory worker or janitor does not need to know chemistry, trigonometry, or Shakespeare, but does need to know basic math, personal finance, and how to get along with coworkers. Students reaching mastery of all basic skills and earning the Basic Diploma would be allowed and encouraged to pursue advanced schooling and therefore receive an Advanced Diploma. Chapter 6 will explain the concepts of the Basic and Advanced Diplomas further.

Problem #3 Lack of relevance: In the Level Mastery System, the required basic skills taught would be limited to those which are *relevant* to most people's lives, i.e. those skills which will enable students to succeed in their future lives.

These are skills such as reading, correct usage of English, spelling, writing, keyboarding, basic math skills, personal finance, job skills, family and home living, parenting skills, healthy living, basic morals, important local, state, and federal laws, the fundamentals of driving, basic manners, effective communicating, and any other skill deemed important by a consensus of U.S. citizens.

Skills and subjects that are required of an Advanced Diploma would be taught in the appropriate secondary academy. For example, a student interested in science and attending the Science and Mathematics Academy might be required to take trigonometry and chemistry, but not Shakespeare or accounting. A student in the Trades Academy, focusing on auto mechanics, might be required to take algebra and physics along with the technical classes, but not philosophy or French. A student in the Fine Arts Academy (including art, music, and theater) might be required to study Shakespeare and art appreciation, but not statistics or anatomy.

Barbara McCombs and James Pope, co-authors of the book Motivating Hard to Reach Students and several other books, assert,

> "*Individuals are naturally motivated to learn…when they perceive what they are learning as being personally meaningful and relevant and when they are in respectful and supportive relationships with teachers.*"[4]

Charles Murray, in Real Education: Four Simple Truths for Bringing America's Schools Back to Reality, writes that

> *"'The forgotten half' is a term used in educational circles to refer to those [students] who are work-bound after high school, not college-bound...The current system makes life as difficult for them as it possibly can. First, high school has been set up so that it provides these students with no incentives to work hard...There are no short-term economic payoffs for good high school grades. So why work hard in high school? Then, high schools ignore the skills that employers of high school graduates do value...people who will show up every day and on time, work hard, and get along with the people around them."*[5]

Murray contends that the "forgotten half" is really more like two-thirds when you include the students who drop out of college before earning a degree. He is concerned that in an effort to encourage everyone to go to college, high schools are actually pushing many of these students to consider dropping out of high school instead of continuing with the one-size-fits-all method of education today. He continues to say,

> *"Worst of all, the current system watches these students approach the age at which they can legally drop out of school and acts as if it wants to push them out, urging them to take more mathematics, language arts, history, and science courses that they don't want to take, so that they can pursue the college chimera."*[6]

The Level Mastery System does not neglect the "forgotten half," but, rather, tailors an education based on each student's personal needs and aspirations, whether that be advanced schooling, vocational training, or simply a Basic Diploma.

Problem #4 Grading and testing: In the Level Mastery System, students would not be allowed to pass on to the next level of a subject until the level they are on is *mastered*, i.e. completed with 100% accuracy, making grades and annual standardized testing unnecessary.

In the present system, businesses hiring high school graduates really have no way of knowing how proficient in certain needed areas those graduates are unless they test them themselves. And we, as a country, have no way of knowing how well our students are being educated because testing only serves to show what the student knows at that point in time, not what they have mastered for life. In the Level Mastery System, students would be required to reach a certain level in each subject to graduate, with the opportunity to move ahead in levels, beyond basic requirements, in order to secure better paying jobs or entrance to better universities or trade schools. In this system, businesses (as well as the rest of society) have only to look at the level of mastery of a student in each subject to know the level of proficiency.

Charles Murray believes, too, that

> *"Young people entering the job market should have a known, trusted measure of their qualifications that they can carry into job interviews. That measure should express what they know and are able to do, not where they learned it or how long it took them to learn it."*[7]

Problem #5 Lack of freedom to learn: In the Level Mastery System, students would have the *freedom* to follow topics that interest them in order to master the basic skills.

Plato, founder of the first institution of higher learning in the western world, instructed,

> *"Do not train children to learning by force and harshness, but direct them to it by what amuses their minds, so that you may be better able to discover with accuracy the peculiar bent of the genius of each."*

So many high school graduates today have no idea what they want to do in the future. Their twenties are spent "finding themselves," which is just an abbreviated way of saying discovering what interests them and what they want to do for the rest of their lives.

Charles Murray states that

> *"The goal of education is to bring children into adulthood having discovered things they enjoy doing and doing them at the outermost limits of their potential."* [8]

The Level Mastery system would allow students the freedom to "find themselves" while they are still in school and to prepare themselves for their future while still in their teen years, thereby allowing them to begin their adult lives in their late teens or early twenties as productive members of society.

Problem #6 Lack of student responsibility: In the Level Mastery System, education would be the *responsibility of the student*. The responsibility of the system would only be to provide the setting and materials for students to *earn* their education.

Students will work at the pace they believe best for them, knowing that the less effort they put into it, the longer it will take them to graduate. There will be little need for teachers to pressure or remind them to get their work done, for the knowledge that many of their peers are moving ahead will eventually spur them to put in more effort. If little or no effort is put into their education, they will not get their Basic Diploma by the age of eighteen and they will be fit only for low-paying and undesirable jobs. On the other hand, students who put a lot of effort into their education will be able to get their Basic Diploma early and pursue an Advanced Diploma, if they so choose.

Since student responsibility has not been emphasized in the current system of education, it may take a couple of years for older students to gain the self-motivation and inspiration to take full responsibility for their education. We may see overall test scores fall for the first couple of years while everyone adjusts to the new system, if Congress insists on continuing standardized testing, to which I am opposed.

Problem #7 Lack of flexibility in the system: Most importantly, the Level Mastery System would be designed so that real changes could be made as needed, including changes to curriculum (mirroring what the public views as important for all adults to know at any given time), structure of education (how students are taught), equipment (books, computers, desks, etc.), structure of the various departments of education, etc.

    To ensure flexibility and to guarantee that local needs and beliefs would be met, I believe it is important to leave the power of day-to-day decision-making at the local level, i.e. district school boards: however, a national framework, a basic structure in effect, would be beneficial to all districts as a place to start.

Six

Basic Structure of the Level Mastery System
(Equine Conformation)

In order to get things started in the right direction, a national framework, or basic structure, of how schools should be set up would be useful. In this chapter, I will explain my vision for a framework for the Level Mastery System.

Entry Level

The first thing a student encounters when entering the current public school system is a lot of structure, rules, and suppression of natural instincts. It is a daunting and sometimes terrifying introduction to the next twelve years of life. I believe this transition from the freedom and security of home to the strictness of school sets many students up to dislike school. Therefore, entry to school should be made as comfortable and welcoming as possible. There are numerous special considerations for Entry Level students that must be addressed in the first couple of years of a student's school career. Some of these are

1. Readiness to learn. As mentioned in Chapter 3, many students are not ready at the age of five to begin formal schooling. Many are too energetic or

immature, either physically, emotionally, or mentally, to benefit from sitting in front of a computer or performing writing tasks. Care must be taken to ensure that these students aren't forced into school before they are ready. Some signs of readiness are

   a. the ability to control and take physical care of the self

   b. the ability to separate easily from the parent/caregiver

   c. the ability to follow directions

   d. fine motor skills needed to use the computer and to handwrite

2. Prior knowledge. Many students have participated in preschool education either in a formal setting, such as a preschool program, or at home with their parents. Others have not had the benefit of such education.

3. The need for a higher teacher-to-student ratio in the entry level. Before students can begin a truly independent learning course, they must be able to read at a basic level, use a computer, and write with some proficiency. Until then, students will need more one-on-one or small group instruction: therefore, more entry-level teachers will be required.

4. Public preschool option. Children who are not ready to enter formal schooling by the age of five or so may need a transition between home and school to prepare them for school. (This is not to be

confused with or used as free day care.) While I advocate children staying home with a parent as long as possible, I realize that this often isn't possible or even desirable in some cases. Many parents must work and cannot stay home with their children; others do not have the education to give their children the skills needed to begin school (though this should be part of the parenting skills taught to all students for future generations). Preschools would focus on allowing the child to mature and develop self control, self sufficiency, ability to separate and follow directions, and fine motor skills, etc., all at the child's own pace. Preschool would be a pleasant, homey atmosphere where every child can feel safe and nurtured, relaxed and comfortable.

The Entry Level, as well, should be a relaxed, enjoyable atmosphere where learning is fun and curiosity is encouraged instead of suppressed. I envision a class of no more than ten to twelve students whose prior knowledge and preparation are similar. Use of the computer would be taught from the first day on so that students can begin using it to learn other skills. Young children are usually quite adept at picking up the necessary computer skills, as anyone who has young children with access to a computer can attest.

The classroom for the Entry Level would resemble a home's family room, with comfortable seating, inviting desk areas, and family-style tables for dining and doing projects. Each student in this level would remain in the same room with the same teacher until he/she is ready to move on to the Basic Level, that is, having reached a specific level of proficiency in both reading and use of the computer.

The educational focus of the Entry Level would be learning to read, using many different methods to achieve this goal. A student may bypass the Entry Level altogether and proceed to the Basic Level if he/she is already proficient in reading and computer use. Students with dyslexia or other learning disabilities which interfere with learning to read would have the time and extra help needed to overcome the disability, if at all possible. A struggling student may stay in the Entry Level for as long as is needed: however, special considerations may be made for a student who, because of disabilities, will probably never become proficient. I believe most students of normal abilities should be able to pass through this level in six months to two years.

Basic Level – the Road to the Basic Diploma

By the time students reach the Basic Level, they will be fairly proficient in reading and using a computer, probably around the ages of six to eight years. In this level, students will work on their own for most of the day. Because of the level of independence, fewer teachers would be required. Students would have individual cubicles with a desk or long tables separated by desk-top dividers, a chair, and a laptop computer with headphones. Several cubicles would be in each room, depending on the size of the room, overseen by one teacher.

The educational focus of the Basic Level would be learning all the skills needed to live a healthy and productive life. These skills would be decided by national consensus and agreed upon by each school district. In this way, we would be sure that the new system reflects what all interested citizens think is important to learn and it also gives our citizens direct involvement and a personal stake in the school system. To obtain a national consensus, a website would be set up for interested citizens of all ages to vote on or enter the skills they feel are important and appropriate for all students to learn.

When the consensus is compiled, local school districts can adapt it to suit their community's lifestyle and values. This is important because communities are different; they have different needs and different experiences. Compare, for example, the lifestyles and educational needs of a student in New York City versus a student in a small Midwestern town. I have long been frustrated with trying to use preschool programs, most of which focus on life in big cities (think of Sesame Street), to teach students in a small rural town. These programs always start out discussing life in a big city neighborhood. In our small town, houses are far apart and there are no "people in your neighborhood" like grocers, repairmen, and bakers. We must drive to a bigger city to encounter those people. Things that are important for students in a big city may not all be the same as the things for students in a small town to learn about. Different geographical areas may have different educational needs, as well. For example, students in the northern states will already know about precipitation in the form of snow, whereas students in the south may need to learn about it. Most of the skills to master, though, will be universal, regardless of geographic differences. A closer look at the general skills I believe are important for all districts is outlined in the next chapter.

Students in the Basic Level would log on to their personalized learning site which would have a summary of the student's progress in each subject. The site would also contain choices for programs and activities for the next level's information in each subject. An example of a personalized progress summary appears in the Appendix, Figure 1. Students would also receive a packet of written activities and projects to choose from. An example of sample contents of a level packet appears in the Appendix, Figure 2.

Near the end of the Basic Level, students should begin to think about how their interests and talents translate into future career choices. Counseling from teacher/mentors, career aptitude tests, and visits to the various local academies and businesses would aid in their decisions.

Advanced Level – Academies for Advanced Diplomas

In the Advanced Level, students would attend a specific academy based on their chosen career path. Examples of these academies include Science and Mathematics Academy (for professions in the sciences, mathematics, medicine, etc.), Languages Academy (for professions in English, journalism, foreign languages, etc.), Social Sciences Academy (for professions in history, geography, government, politics, philosophy, etc.), Business and Economics Academy (for professions in management, marketing, economics, etc.), Trades Academy (for professions such as electrician, plumber, auto mechanic, etc.), and Arts Academy (for professions in art, music, theater, etc.). In school districts which have more than one high school, academies could be set up with one or two per building. In smaller districts or in ones in which transportation costs are a factor, one building could house all the academies: however, an effort should made to have some sort of physical separation of the academies such as one academy per floor or wing, if possible, to foster a sense of cohesiveness for each academy.

Having chosen an academy at the completion of the Basic Level, students would be assigned a cubicle, which they would keep throughout their tenure in that academy, unless a change is requested by the student or teacher. This provides students with a sense of continuity and more closely resembles a real-life work situation.

Curricula in the Advanced Level would be geared toward a particular career path and the learning of such would be regarded as a student's job. As in the Basic Level, most learning would be done independently by each student with occasional small group assignments. Each student would have an opportunity to intern, or apprentice, at a local business which most closely relates to the student's chosen future profession for at least a semester, ideally more than one semester.

Classroom Layout

As in the Basic Level, each student would be provided with a cubicle including a desk (or a table with dividers), a laptop computer with headphones, a comfortable chair, and storage drawers and/or shelves. Each student would have the ability to personalize his/her own cubicle. In the center of the room, there would be tables for dining and doing activities. Students would bring their own chairs to the table as needed. The teacher/mentor assigned to each class would also have a cubicle (though probably larger than the students' desks) equipped with a computer, drawers, shelves, etc. There would be one or more printers in each classroom to print things as needed. Samples of classroom layouts appear in the Appendix, Figures 3 and 4.

Daily Routines

Keeping in mind that the most important component of any new system of education must be flexibility, a loosely defined routine for daily activity is, nonetheless, beneficial for maintaining flow and cohesion. A daily routine may include school beginning and ending times, time for lunch, and time for whole school activities, such as exercise or assemblies. The routine would *not* define explicit times for working on specific subjects or taking bathroom and rest breaks: these would be under the control of each student.

Teacher Responsibilities

Each teacher's responsibilities would include assembling an education program personalized for each student, mentoring and supporting students, maintaining discipline (always encouraging self-discipline), giving level mastery assessments, and various administrative duties.

A personalized education program would consist of loading each student's laptop with links to educational software programs that fit the levels and various interests of each student. The software programs would be made available for school use by the national Department of Education through universal software licensing. Each personalized program would also include a packet of tangible worksheets, games, and other projects for students to do, if they so choose. This packet of materials would be personalized to each student's level and interest, so getting to know each student's interests is a vital responsibility for the teacher, as well. A sample of the contents of a level packet and software links can be found in the Appendix, Figure 2.

Student Responsibilities

In this system, students would have the greatest amount of responsibility in their own education. From the very beginning of their school careers, students would be responsible for choosing what skills to work on at any given time and in which way to learn those skills. Early on, students would naturally gravitate toward subjects that interest them and, gradually, would discover the ways they learn best. Students would have the responsibility of communicating their interests and needs to their teachers. Students and teachers would form a partnership, with students expressing their educational needs and interests to teachers and teachers finding material suitable for allowing students to fulfill those needs.

Another responsibility of students would be to let the teacher know when they are ready to be assessed for a particular level or skill. The term "assess" is used purposely here instead of "test" as it infers merely an evaluation of what has been learned, not a judgment of how well the student was listening or how much studying was done. An assessment should be something students look forward to, as a way to advance, not as a way to be criticized and graded or compared to other students. Assessments would be non-threatening, un-timed, one-on-one with the teacher, a combination of written and oral answers, and maybe a computer application. For example, an assessment for a basic math level may include the student working some addition problems on paper, then explaining to the teacher how he/she came up with each answer, then playing an addition racing game on the computer. If the student makes a mistake but knows why and is able to fix it, he/she would be allowed to do so. If the student cannot fix the mistake or doesn't understand why it is wrong, the teacher would encourage him/her to go back and practice some more on those skills. When the teacher and student are both confident that the student has mastered these skills, the student is passed on to the next level. The teacher then loads new links into the student's computer and provides a new packet of materials for that level.

Of course, with each student receiving a laptop computer to use at school or at home, an enormous responsibility for the care and safekeeping of said computer would belong to each student. Our current system entrusts textbooks, library books, paper handouts, etc., to students throughout the school year, all adding up to a specific cost, all or most of which can be concentrated into the cost of the laptop in this new system. Insurance would cover verifiable thefts and disasters, but students (and their parents) would be held responsible for negligence, willful misconduct, and suspicious thefts. After one such incident, the student concerned would be able to use a computer only while at school, instead of being able to take it off-campus.

Students would also be responsible for keeping their cubicles and classrooms clean and orderly. While teachers would be responsible for cleaning up their own personal areas and for supervising janitorial duties for the common classroom areas, students would be the ones to perform the duties for their own areas and common areas. Outside the classroom, students would also have responsibilities and duties to care for the rest of the school property – things such as picking up trash in the schoolyard and hallways, dumping wastebaskets, sweeping the hall floors, etc. Students could also be put to work planting flower gardens, painting walls, doors and trim, and otherwise beautifying their school. In this way, students will gain respect for and pride in their school, as well as learning valuable skills to make their lives easier and more productive in the future, as nearly everyone will need to maintain their own living areas in their adult lives. This is not to be considered slave labor but an opportunity for students to learn valuable living skills and responsibility.

The responsibility for feeding students would also rest with the students themselves. Students will be encouraged to make and bring their own lunches and snacks from home. Parents will have the responsibility of providing the food and supervising young children in making their lunches, but even a five-year-old can make a sandwich, bag some carrot sticks, and choose a fruit for lunch. And, of course, students would be responsible for cleaning up after lunch.

One of the most important responsibilities students will undertake is to figure out what they want to do after they earn the Basic Diploma. Giving students the responsibility of making this choice will eliminate much of the anger and dissatisfaction that we see in teenagers today. Since the choice for their future and the consequences of that choice are laid directly in their laps, they are forced to take ownership for their future and have no one to blame but themselves if it goes awry. By the time they receive their Basic Diploma, they will be used to taking responsibility and steering the course of their education. In the current system, they can blame their teachers, the irrelevance of the subjects taught, the help they did not receive, the stifling atmosphere of school, etc. for their failures in life. In the Level Mastery System, this is impossible: all choices are made by the students: all achievements and all failures belong solely to them.

Stop Beating the Dead Horse

Seven

Curriculum for the Basic Diploma
(Learning to Ride Your New Horse)

As mentioned in Chapter 6, the curriculum for the Basic Diploma would be developed at the national level and decided upon by a consensus of U.S. citizens. The word *curriculum* is used loosely here; instead of its normal definition as "a course of study," what is really meant is a set of skills. These skills, not the subjects used to learn the skills, must be mastered for a student to receive the Basic Diploma. For example, instead of specifying that a student must take and pass a course in arithmetic, skills such as *adding, subtracting,* and *being able to figure percentages* would be stipulated. A student who is interested in baseball may choose to learn those skills by keeping baseball statistics and he or she may not be ready to learn those skills until the age of, say, twelve – well past the age when students are currently required to learn them. Or the student may be eager and ready to learn them at five or six. In the end, it is not important *when* or *how* the skills are learned but, rather, *how well* they are learned and that they are mastered for life.

When one considers which skills to include in the Basic Diploma, the most important criterion to remember is that each skill should be one that is significant to all (or, at least, most) citizens, regardless of their careers, religious preferences, station in life, etc. These skills should make life easier for people; they should enable each person to make informed choices, to be independent and to be in control of their lives – financially, politically, socially, medically, etc. All the practical skills that adults, in retrospect, wish they had learned in school, such as home mortgage options or cooking healthy meals, should be included. Skills and attitudes that businesses desire in an employee, such as good communication, reliability, responsibility, dependability, creativity, good work ethic, and good attitude should be cultivated.

Many of these skills are outlined in current GLE (grade level expectation) requirements. However, some of the GLEs do not meet the criterion mentioned above and so do not need to be included in the Basic Diploma. Providing a way for all interested citizens to vote on those skills they believe to be important, as the website mentioned in chapter 6 does, ensures that the Basic Diploma will serve the needs of people of all ages and all walks of life. An example of such a website is in Chapter 10, Figure 5.

Again, remember that these skills are the ones required for only the Basic Diploma. More advanced and subject-specific skills and knowledge will be required to obtain an advanced diploma. In this way, we ensure that all our citizens have the basic skills needed to live happy and successful lives, while also allowing students who have the talent and aspiration to advance their education to the level they desire. I believe this will increase test scores in all areas because each student will be tested on information they find directly relevant to their lives.

Below is listed a synopsis of the skills I believe to be important to include in the Basic Diploma. Special considerations may be needed for students with learning disabilities: perhaps a specialized diploma or a noted exception on the Basic Diploma. The skills I have chosen may or may not be what the majority of U.S. citizens deem important. That is why I propose the national consensus, so that no single person or special interest group makes these important decisions. In this way, the entire nation feels a personal responsibility to our education system.

Skills for the Basic Diploma

Reading Skills

Being able to read at a minimum of an eighth grade level

Language Skills

Being able to use English effectively and correctly when writing or speaking, including being able to spell words correctly

Being able to use language resources such as a dictionary and thesaurus

Being able to print and write cursive legibly

Computer Skills

Being able to type and use a computer mouse

Being able to use search engines for research

Mathematics Skills

Being able to perform basic mathematical skills

Being able to perform basic algebraic skills

Being able to perform measurements primarily using the metric system

Science Skills

Being able to understand basic science concepts, such as the scientific process, the cycle of life, and basic physics

Being able to make informed conclusions about scientific discoveries and research

Social Studies Skills

Being able to recall major eras and events in human history and understand their impact on civilization

Being able to locate major geographical features such as the continents, countries, bodies of water, mountain ranges, etc. on a map or globe

Being familiar with local, state, and national laws and regulations

Being able to pass the citizenship exam

Life Skills

Being able to live and work compatibly with others

Being able to parent a child effectively

Being able to maintain a household

Being able to prepare healthy meals

Being able to keep oneself healthy through exercise and proper diet

Being able perform personal finance tasks such as balancing a checkbook, opening a bank account, paying bills, managing personal credit report, negotiating a reasonable mortgage, making sound investments, etc.

Being able to understand the concepts and physics of safe driving

Character Skills

Being able to identify universally accepted morals such as prohibitions from murdering, stealing, lying, and cheating, etc.

Being able to distinguish between right and wrong and to deliberate situations in which the distinction is not clear

Being able to recognize and exhibit positive character traits such as honesty, integrity, respect, responsibility, fairness, diligence, self-discipline, courage, perseverance, independence, etc.

Eight

Curricula for the Advanced Diploma
(Now You're Ready for the Show)

After earning the Basic Diploma, students who are under the age of majority (i.e., eighteen, in most states), will be eligible to attend an academy in order to earn an Advanced Diploma. Students who wish to go to college or to learn skills for a specific career will probably choose to attend a particular academy. Students who feel they know all they need to know to pass the exams to enter college or to begin a career may choose to bypass the Advanced Diploma. For example, a student who wants a career as a factory worker, a custodian, or a retail clerk may not need the skills taught in an academy; therefore, she may decide that her education is complete. Other students may have the opportunity to learn their chosen craft on the job, such as an apprenticeship for a trade, making an Advanced Diploma unnecessary. Still other students – the brightest and most motivated – may already possess enough knowledge to pass entrance exams and, thus, may go on to college without attending an academy. If, however, any of these students change their minds, they may enroll in an academy at any time as long as they are under the age of majority.

The curriculum for each Advanced Diploma would also consist of skills and may also require fact-based knowledge. Those skills and facts would be chosen by a consensus of people involved in that particular field. For example, the skills and knowledge base for an Advanced Diploma in Science would be decided on by those employed in the medical and science fields, for an Advanced Diploma in Theater by actors and employers of actors, for an Advanced Diploma in Auto Mechanics by professional auto mechanics. Since the students in any academy have already mastered basic skills, they can now focus on the skills and knowledge necessary for a future career. In the example of the Science Academy, skills and knowledge such as advanced sciences, advanced mathematics, advanced communication skills, and any specialized skills identified by the professionals in science fields would have to be mastered in order to receive the Advanced Diploma in Science. For an Advanced Diploma in Theater, the skills and knowledge may include reading Shakespeare and other important playwrights, cultivation of the voice, acting, lighting, makeup, costuming, and stage management.

In Chapter 4, the case is made against using a liberal arts curriculum for the Basic Diploma. Also mentioned, however, is that some of the Advanced Diplomas, in particular some college preparatory ones, would require a curriculum that more resembles a liberal arts curriculum – one that consists of classes such as literature, philosophy, geometry, astronomy, music, etc. Students who are on track to pursue a bachelor of arts degree are generally able to succeed in these classes; in fact, they are the students who naturally gravitate toward these subjects. Think of the smartest person you knew in high school. Chances are this person excelled in science and mathematics, read many high-brow books such as Tolstoy's <u>War and Peace</u>, enjoyed discussing philosophical points of view and arguing the logic of a particular process, and played a musical instrument, often the violin. These things are the epitome of a liberal arts curriculum, and as you can probably see, they are not for everyone. Usually, only the brightest minds are excited by and excel in this atmosphere. For everyone else, it is tedious and off-putting. Charles Murray writes

> "*Getting a liberal education consists of dealing with complex intellectual material day after day, and... is what students in the top few percentiles are really good at, in the same way that other people are really good at cooking or making pottery.*"[1]

Students who want to pursue a bachelor of science or a trade may not want to take on a complete liberal arts repertoire, and that shouldn't be a requirement. Requiring extraneous courses which have nothing to do with a student's interests or future endeavors would simply create boredom, apathy, and, worst of all, antipathy.

Stop Beating the Dead Horse

Nine

Financing the Level Mastery System
(Betting on the New Horse)

The Level Mastery System would save money for the country in many ways. Most significantly, the budget for the Department of Education (ED) can be drastically reduced, as it would no longer need many of the departments it currently has – such as the Office of Vocational and Adult Education, the Office of English Language Acquisition, or the Office of Migrant Education – since the Level Mastery System naturally tailors an education to suit the needs of each individual. The ED employs about 4200 bureaucrats and has a budget of almost 64 billion dollars a year. [1] Between 2002 and 2005, the department's budget increased 70%, yet education of students in the United States has not improved accordingly.[2] In fact, many studies show that spending more money on education does not translate into better education.

In The Conspiracy of Ignorance: The Failure of the American Public Schools, Martin L. Gross reports, *"In inflation-adjusted dollars, we are now spending two to three times more per child than in 1960, when performance was generally higher."*[3] Gross reminds his readers that parochial schools generally have higher academic performance while spending 40 percent less per pupil than public schools. He points out that much of the increase in public school costs can be attributed to the explosion in non-teacher employees such as administrators, support personnel, and bureaucrats. The number of support personnel, including reading specialists, teacher's aides, guidance counselors, etc. has increased fourfold since 1960. Gross states, *"Overall, there is now an army of more than five million school personnel, one for every* nine *students."*[4] Of course, a number of staff positions will still be needed, especially for special needs students, but the overall amount of staff positions could be reduced drastically with the Level Mastery System since each student would be receiving individualized instruction tailored to fit his/her needs.

Reducing the number of bureaucratic positions in the ED, as well as the various state departments of education, would translate into a major reduction in the cost of education while increasing the amount of money directly available for students. There seems to be an inverse correlation between the amount of money put into the Department of Education and the performance of students in the system. In reality, though, test scores of students in mathematics and reading have pretty much stayed the same since 1971, according to the National Assessment of Educational Progress (NAEP) data, despite the massive amounts of money poured into education since then. The reason we perceive that the education of our citizens is getting worse is because countries whose educational systems lagged behind ours in the past are ever improving and surpassing ours, while we have stayed at the same level for at least forty years. And the reason we've stayed the same is that we've used the same system of education, with changes and improvements implemented only as they fit into the existing system and billions of dollars spent to shore up that system. No matter how much money is put into the system, it is still the same system – a system that is contrary to the way students learn best. The old adages "you can't make a silk purse out of a sow's ear," and "throwing good money after bad" apply appropriately here.

In the Level Mastery System, the ED would serve one major purpose – setting up and maintaining a national framework for the new system. This framework consists of several parts:

1. Creating and managing a website for obtaining a consensus of basic skills,

2. Compiling the votes and creating the requirements for the Basic Diploma and updating them on a regular basis,

3. Polling businesses to determine the requirements for each type of Advanced Diploma,

4. Contracting computer software companies to create a wide variety of educational software to promote learning the basic skills, and obtaining a universal license for each piece of software,

5. Creating and maintaining a web-based resource list for teachers to use in creating personalized education programs for each student,

6. Obtaining bulk pricing for laptop computers, e-books, and any other universally needed item

The ED's role in education would be limited to those things that directly benefit students, instead of making policies, conducting studies, writing memos, and other things that never trickle down to the improvement of individual student education. It's reasonable to assume that most teachers, students, and even most citizens do not know exactly what the current ED does to benefit the education of our students. Certainly, the ED and the billions of dollars it has spent since its inception in 1980 have not improved education: test scores have not increased, but problems like school violence, teen pregnancies, and drop-out rates have. Clearly, the current ED is not set up to directly improve the system. It needs to be replaced, as well.

Another way that the Level Mastery System would save taxpayer money while improving education is by focusing on academics and leaving non-academic, extra-curricular activities such as sports, social clubs, and social mixers to other organizations. School gymnasiums can be used for academics and/or leased to organizations after school hours for activities. There is no doubt that other organizations, such as the YMCA, church groups, social clubs, or associations formed specifically for an activity would provide opportunities for these activities. They already fill in for activities not offered at schools, such as sports associations, dance and gymnastic centers, theater groups, and youth groups. In that way, the participants and their families pay directly for an activity instead of all taxpayers funding it for the few who are involved. Community support and attendance to events could also help fund clubs. In this way, taxes for all would be decreased, allowing extra room in a family's budget to pay for desired non-academic activities.

Eliminating the school lunch program would save taxpayers approximately 9.3 billion dollars annually (figures from 2008).[5] It also frees up a large room (i.e. the school cafeteria) to use for academics. Shifting the responsibility of feeding students to the families and to the students themselves not only saves money, but also instills the desirable qualities of self sufficiency and responsibility while teaching the skills of food selection, acquisition, and preparation. Families who cannot or will not provide food for their children would be referred to family services for assistance in parenting skills, budgeting, food stamps if eligible, etc.

The costs involved with textbooks, a large percentage of paper and copying costs, and school libraries filled with books would be virtually eliminated, as most of these would be replaced with computer-based instruction. As an avid reader, I find the thought of replacing a library of tangible books with digital books somewhat distressing; however, many citizens do not realize the enormous costs involved with stocking and maintaining a school library. Many states have guidelines which require that schools replace books whose copyrights are more than a few years old, even if the new book is exactly the same as the old one. Also, many books must be replaced often due to outdated information or new restrictions on subject matter. School libraries can be made more efficient and cost-effective by switching to digital books (e-books), loaded onto a student's laptop computer at his or her request. A computer can hold thousands of e-books in a very small space, whereas the same number of conventional books requires a large amount of space and physical care. Having e-books instead of conventional books also eases students' backpack load and the problem of losing or damaging books. There are thousands of free e-books available for download and for those that are not free, deals could be sought with e-book publishers to allow downloads of an unlimited number of e-books for an annual set fee, saving taxpayers even more money.

Remediation costs school districts a lot of money, as well. Students who have missed vital information and skills must get additional tutoring outside the regular classroom in order to catch up with the rest of the students. In many cases, the costs of tutoring falls on the parents, who have already paid taxes to a system that is supposed to adequately educate their children. In the Level Mastery System, students would never need remediation, as they are always working on the level directly above that which has been mastered. They will never miss vital information nor will they move on until full understanding of the level is achieved. This will carry over into college as well; students who are pursuing a college track in secondary school will be prepared to start college courses without the need for remedial courses. The costs of remediation to institutions of higher education will be reduced greatly, if not eliminated entirely.

The most important financial benefit of the Level Mastery System is in the improved education of all our citizens. No longer will huge financial crises threaten our public welfare. No longer will it be easy for greedy shysters take advantage of large numbers of under-educated people. No longer will politicians conveniently impose their self-serving agendas on our uninformed populace. No longer will the United States be embarrassed in international academic competition. Informed and educated citizens will be equipped to take control of their financial lives and political interests. Students who are well prepared and passionate about their chosen field of study will fare far better in academic competitions. The United States will again be able to draw on its vast resources to become a major supplier in world commerce instead of just the number one consumer. Our citizens, for the most part, would likely become independent, responsible, and moral again, as were our ancestors who shaped this country. These qualities translate into fewer drug problems, fewer people needing welfare, and less need for law enforcement.

The author is aware that this all sounds idealistic, especially coming from a hard-core realist such as I. However, I truly believe that the vast majority of our nation's problems can be solved, or at least greatly alleviated, through the right system of education: a system which allows individuality and requires independent responsibility, while at the same time fostering joy and enthusiasm for learning. The fact that our current system misses so many opportunities for addressing existing problems is disgraceful. As the Roman slave and philosopher Epictetus said, *"Only the educated are free."* It is time to provide a system of education that allows our citizens to become truly educated, not just filled with facts, but able to think for themselves. Only then can we become truly free to run our lives and contribute to society in a way that maximizes benefits for us all.

Stop Beating the Dead Horse

Ten

How to Get Started
(First, Place Your Foot in the Stirrup)

The Level Mastery System can address all the problems in the current system of education as well as many of the problems people are facing in their lives today. It can also be changed as needed for any future developments in our educational needs. What we need to get started is for citizens to urge lawmakers to make real changes to the system of education, not just throw more money and rhetoric at the dead horse. The changes must be made from the top down – from the voters to Congress, to the Education Department, to state education departments, then to local school districts, and, finally, to the students themselves.

Specifically, once Congress has made the decision to change, the first things that need to be done are at the national level: set up a website to get a national consensus for the basic skills, poll business leaders to find out what needs to be included in the requirements for each Advanced Diploma, contract for software programs and obtain universal licensing, create a web-based resource list for teachers, procure laptop computers, etc.

Once the Education Department has these things set up, state departments of education, then local districts and individual schools can begin to set up their programs and tailor the national framework to suit their local needs and values.

So what is there for you and me, ordinary citizens of the United States, to do? We have the most important duty of all: to discard our apathy and blind adherence to a system which does not educate our nation's children effectively and to reach out to our elected officials – local, state, and federal – to let them know, both verbally and by our votes, that we want a real change to the system, i.e. a new system, that we will not allow this beating of a "dead horse" to continue any longer.

Appendices

Figure 1	Sample Personalized Progress Summary
Figure 2	Sample Contents of Level Packet and Corresponding Software Links
Figure 3	Sample Classroom Layout 1
Figure 4	Sample Classroom Layout 2
Figure 5	Sample Website for Voting on Basic Diploma Curriculum

Stop Beating the Dead Horse

Figure 1

Sample Personalized Progress Summary

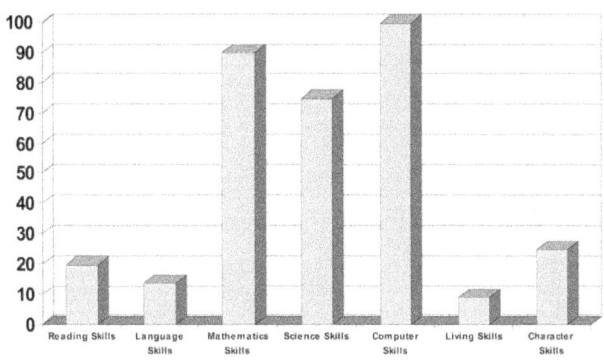

This progress summary shows that Johnny has reached the highest level of mastery in computer skills and is well on his way to achieving the highest levels in mathematics skills and science skills, as well. He has quite a way to go in the other skills, so he will be spending more of his productive time on those subjects in the future. Once he has achieved the highest level in all skills, he will receive his Basic Diploma and be eligible for graduation or placement in an Academy for an Advanced Diploma.

Stop Beating the Dead Horse

Figure 2

Sample Contents of Level Packet and Corresponding Software Links

Level One Reading

SKILLS TO MASTER:
Identify letters in the alphabet
Identify the sound(s) each letter makes

WORKSHEETS AND ACTIVITIES:
Alphabet worksheets
Alphabet blocks
Alphabet puzzles
Alphabet games

COMPUTER WORK:
Phonics - Starfall.com
Between the Lions - pbskids.org/lions
Interactive Storybooks - teacher.scholastic.com
GameGoo - earobics.com/gamegoo/gooey.html

BOOKS:
Bob Books for Beginning Readers by Bobby Lynn Maslen
Dr. Seuss Beginning Readers books

Stop Beating the Dead Horse

Figure 3 Sample Classroom Layout (room for 20 students)

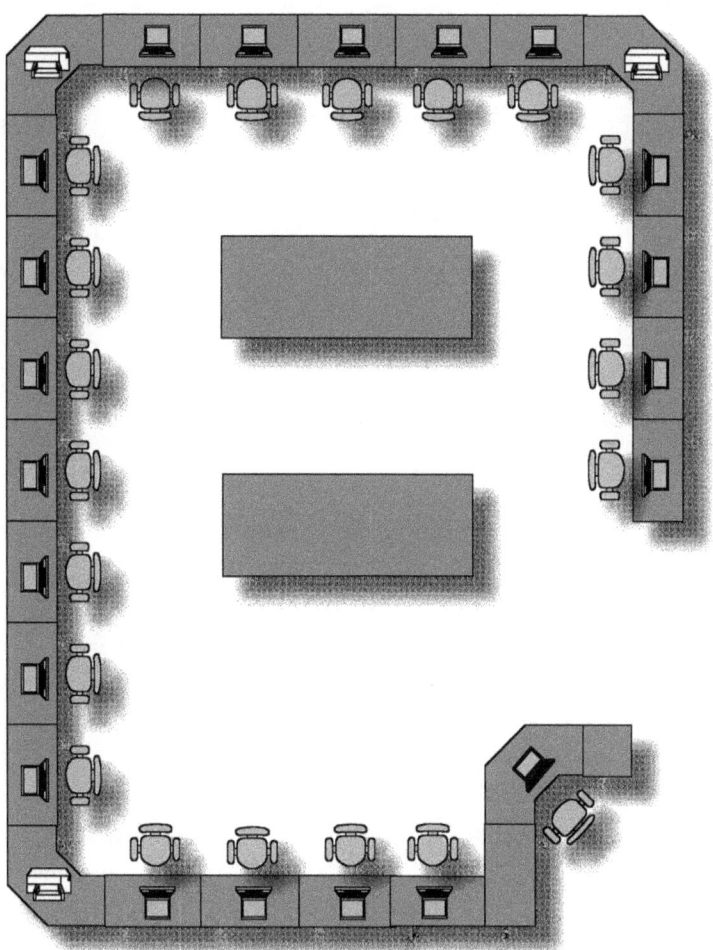

Stop Beating the Dead Horse

Stop Beating the Dead Horse

Figure 4 Sample Classroom Layout (room for 20 students)

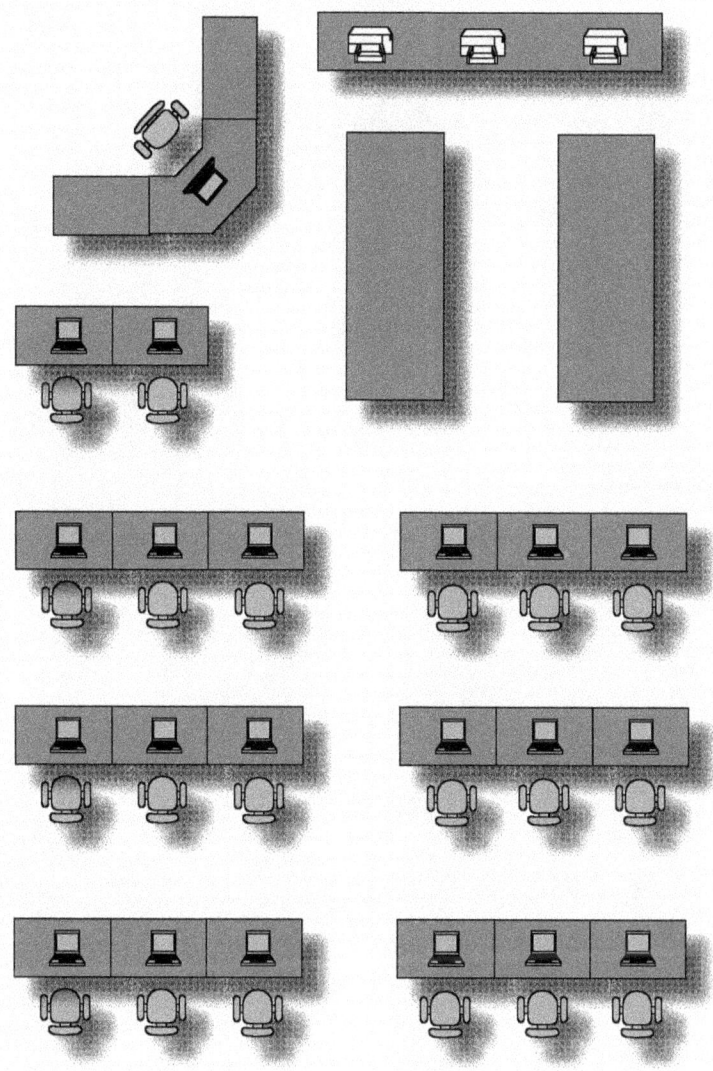

Stop Beating the Dead Horse

Figure 5 Sample Website for Voting on Basic Diploma

Make your choices by clicking on the circle which best describes how important you feel each skill is for students to learn for the Basic Diploma in Language Arts:

Very Important	Somewhat Important	Not Important	Undesirable	
○	●	○	○	Being able to name and describe the parts of speech (e.g. noun, verb, adjective)
●	○	○	○	Being able to use the parts of speech correctly when speaking
○	○	○	●	Being able to use slang words effectively when speaking
●	○	○	○	Being able to compose a coherent letter, memo, or story
●	○	○	○	Being able to spell the most commonly used words correctly
●	○	○	○	Being able to read at a fourth grade level
●	○	○	○	Being able to read at a sixth grade level
○	●	○	○	Being able to read at an eighth grade level
●	○	○	○	Being able to punctuate written sentences correctly

References

Chapter 1

1 Murray, Charles, <u>Real Education: Four Simple Truths for Bringing America's School Back to Reality</u>, Crown Forum, New York, NY, 2008, p. 153.

2 Gatto, John Taylor, "Speech to the Vermont Homeschooling Conference," http://4brevard.com/choice/Public_Education.htm.

Chapter 2

1 Gatto, John Taylor, "Speech to the Vermont Homeschooling Conference," http://4brevard.com/choice/Public_Education.htm.

2 Fuller, Cheri, "Early Schooling: An Idea Whose Time Has Gone?" <u>Southwest Policy Institute Policy Study</u>, No. 2, 1989. p. 3.

3 Backpack Buddies program, http://backpack-buddies.org/.

4 Dawn Rizzoni, CNSNews.com, "Study Finds Homeschooled Children Better at Social Skills," http://www.comeover.to/homeschool/socialsskills.htm.

5 Stough, L. (1992), "Social and Emotional Status of Homeschooled Children and Conventionally Schooled Children in West Virginia," M.S. Thesis, University of West Virginia. *[ED 353079]*, <u>Homeschooling and Socialization of Children</u>, ERIC digests: http:/www.ed.gov/database/ERIC_digests/ed372460.html.

6 Gross, Martin L, The Conspiracy of Ignorance: The Failure of the American Public Schools, HarperCollins Publishers, Inc., New York, NY, 1999, pp. 191-192.

7 Epstein, Robert, Ph.D., The Case Against Adolescence: Rediscovering the Adult in Every Teen, Quill Driver Books, Sanger, CA, 2007.

8 "Special Analysis: Teen Pregnancy: Trends And Lessons Learned," The Guttmacher Report on Public Policy, February 2002, Volume 5, Number 1, Guttmacher Institute, 2008.

9 Cohen, Elizabeth, "CDC: Antidepressants Most Prescribed Drugs in U.S.," CNN Health.com http://www.cnn.com/2007/HEALTH/07/09/antidepressants/index.html

10 "The Employment Situation: December 2008," Bureau of Labor Statistics, U.S. Department of Labor, http://www.bls.gov/news.release/archives/empsit_01092009.htm.

11 "Most Young People Entering the U.S. Workforce Lack Critical Skills Essential for Success," The Partnership for 21st Century Skills, http://21stcenturyskills.org/index.php?option=com_content&task=view&id=250&Itemid=64.

12 "Operation Iraqi Freedom and Operation Enduring Freedom Casualties," icasualties.org, http://www.icasualties.org.

13 "Motor vehicle traffic deaths," and "All firearm deaths," FastStats, Centers for Disease Control and Prevention, http://www.cdc.gov/nchs/fastats/injury.htm.

14 Tyre, Peg, The Trouble with Boys, Crown Publishers, New York, 2008, p. 111.

15 Schrag, Peter and Diane Divoky, The Myth of the Hyperactive Child, Pantheon Books, New York, 1975, pp. xii-xiii.

16 Schrag and Divoky, p. xv.

17 "Retirement Income: Implications of Demographic Trends for Social Security and Pension Reform," Washington, D.C.: U.S. Government Printing Office, 1997, p. 47.

18 "Licensed Drivers and Vehicle Registrations," Infoplease, http://www.infoplease.com/ipa/A0908125.html.

Chapter 3

1 Tyre, Peg, The Trouble with Boys, Crown Publishers, New York, 2008, p 55.

2 Finn, Chester E., Jr., and Diane Ravitch, "Is Educational Reform a Failure?, USA Today Magazine, November 1996.

3 Gross, Martin L, The Conspiracy of Ignorance: The Failure of the American Public Schools, HarperCollins Publishers, Inc., New York, NY, 1999, p. 17.

4 Schneider, Jeremy, Chalkbored: What's Wrong with School & How to Fix It, Pace of Mind, 2007, p. 11.

5 Schneider, p. 7.

6 Schneider, p. 192.

Chapter 4

1 "Winnetka Plan," <u>Britannica Online</u>, http://www.eb.com:180/cgi-bin/g?DocF=micro/709/43.html.

2 Davis, Denese, and Sorrell, Jackie, "Mastery Learning in Public Schools," <u>Educational Psychology Interactive</u>, Valdosta, GA: Valdosta Statue University, 1995.

Chapter 5

1 Chugach School District, http://www.chugachschools.com.

2 Adams 50 School District, http://www.sbsadams50.org/content/.

3 "Should schools do away with age-dependent grade levels?" http://www.parade.com/news/intelligence-report/archive/the-end-of-grade-levels.html.

4 McCombs, Barbara, and James Pope, <u>Motivating Hard to Reach Students</u>, American Psychological Association, Washington, D.C., 1994.

5 Murray, Charles, <u>Real Education: Four Simple Truths for Bringing America's School Back to Reality</u>, Crown Forum, New York, NY, 2008, pp. 147-148.

6 Murray, p. 149.

7 Murray, p. 156.

8 Murray, p. 168.

Chapter 8

1 Murray, pp. 82-83.

Chapter 9

1 "About ED - Overview," U.S. Department of Education Website, http://www2.ed.gov/about/landing.jhtml?src=gu.

2 "Education Department Budget History Table," U.S. Department of Education Website, http://www2.ed.gov/about/overview/budget/history/edhistory.pdf.

3 Gross, Martin L, <u>The Conspiracy of Ignorance: The Failure of the American Public Schools</u>, HarperCollins Publishers, Inc., New York, NY, 1999, p. 30.

4 Gross, p. 31.

5 "National School Lunch Program," http://www.fns.usda.gov/cnd/lunch/AboutLunch/NSLPFactsheet.pdf.

About the Author

Julie Casey lives in a rural area near St. Joseph, Missouri, with her husband, a high school science teacher and three youngest sons. Ms. Casey has a B.S. Ed in Elementary Education and a B.S. in Computer Programming/Analysis. After teaching preschool for fifteen years, she has been homeschooling her four sons for ten years.

Find out more at www.julielcasey.com.

A Message from the author:

Thank you for taking the time to read my book. I would be honored if you would consider leaving a review for it on ***Amazon***.

Check out these titles from
Amazing Things Press

Guardians of Holt by Julie L. Casey
Keeper of the Mountain by Nshan Erganian
Rare Blood Sect by Robert L. Justus
Evoloving by James Fly
Survival In the Kitchen by Sharon Boyle
Stop Beating the Dead Horse by Julie L. Casey
In Daddy's Hands by Julie L. Casey
Time Lost: Teenage Survivalist II by Julie L. Casey

www.amazingthingspress.com

www.ingramcontent.com/pod-product-compliance
Lightning Source LLC
Chambersburg PA
CBHW071510040426
42444CB00008B/1578